ENLIGHTENED DESPOTISM

EUROPE SINCE 1500: *A Paperbound Series*

ENLIGHTENED DESPOTISM

John G. Gagliardo

BOSTON UNIVERSITY

THOMAS Y. CROWELL COMPANY

NEW YORK / ESTABLISHED 1834

For My Mother

Preface

The phrase "Enlightened Despotism" came into existence in the works of nineteenth-century historians as an unproved assumption about a certain period of European history in the eighteenth century. It would not be an exaggeration to say that much of the history of the phrase since its inception has revolved around the attempt to find out whether it means anything and, if so, exactly what. In 1928, at the behest of a prominent French historian, an international committee of historians set itself the task of examining "Enlightened Despotism," with the end of determining if there was such a thing after all—or, putting it another way, of ascertaining just what the historical period called the Enlightenment actually had to do with "despots" who were "enlightened" or with anything else that might justify the internal consistency of that period of history.

The work of this commission over the decade of its existence contributed much valuable information to serve as a basis for further study. So have the researches and conclusions of numerous other scholars who have written on the subject since. But there is still a need for a short synthetic survey or examination of Enlightened Despotism; this is so not merely because of many still unexplored interpretative aspects of the topic, but also because much recent work concerned with it has been scattered and as yet unincorporated in any general survey. This book is intended to supply that need.

In the face of the numerous disagreements among historians concerning the meaning and applicability of the term "Enlightened Despotism," the only thing continuing to give form to the controversy is the existence of certain points of common agreement that constitute a framework for continuing debate. Thus, virtually all historians agree that in its specific application, "Enlightened Despotism" refers to a period of European history corresponding roughly with the three decades or so preceding the French Revolution, i.e., the period 1760 to 1790. Most would agree further that this period appears in certain respects to possess an internal cohesion that lends it a relatively distinct unity; that this cohesion relates primarily to the internal policies of numerous monarchical states of Europe, characterized during this time by more or less vigorous reform activity; and that this reform activity, with respect both to motivation and goals, presents certain features suggesting one or another degree of influence by the philosophic and humanitarian movement known as the Enlightenment.

But here agreement stops; historians who are willing to use "Enlightened Despotism" as a shorthand expression for a period or for a problem are not necessarily willing to use it as a ready-made solution to the problem. And as it stands, the term does contain a solution—namely, the assumption that the consistency connecting the reforms of the various states in this period, and therefore giving unity to the entire period, lies in the fact of major influence of "enlightened" ideas or ideals on the "despots" who decreed the reforms. This assumption is not permissible, for it begs the entire question of the nature and meaning of the period concerned. It must be insisted that, while it may be desirable to accept provisionally the common points of agreement expressed in the previous paragraph as others have, this is done only for purposes of argument and to establish certain reference points— "straw men," perhaps—which provide the springboard, not the finish line, for an investigation that must ultimately involve questioning the validity of all of them. Thus, Enlightened Despotism does not yet belong among those historical subjects for the writing of descriptive histories; it remains an historical problem, which must be approached and written about as such.

The subject to be dealt with in this book is a broad one. It would be broader still without two specific limitations we have imposed: first, we will not treat foreign policy or international relations, whose examination would require more space than this short study permits; second, we will exclude from the scope of the book such states as England, Holland, and Switzerland, whose political character differed substantially from those of the absolute monarchies of Europe. In both cases, it would be possible to draw some interesting and suggestive conclusions that would further round out the picture of enlightened despotism to emerge in the following pages; but it is fair to say that no serious deficiencies in the treatment of the topic will result from their exclusion.

In the final analysis, it is the reforms of the monarchs of the period that must be at the center of investigation; the nature of these reforms, with respect to motivation, purposes, and effects, is what will finally determine the character of the period to which the label "Enlightened Despotism" has been applied for so long. Scarcely less important for purposes of analysis, however, in view not only of past interpretations but also of direct evidence from the period, is the vast intellectual movement we know as the Enlightenment, whose representatives and publicists in the eighteenth century itself were only the first in a long line of observers to suggest the influence of philosophy on the reform programs of monarchs throughout Europe. It will therefore be appropriate to begin our investigation with a brief description of the enlightened temper of the age into which reform was to be introduced.

Finally, I would like to express my appreciation to the Research Board of the University of Illinois for making available funds for the employment of a research assistant to help in the compilation of some of the materials for this book. My thanks go also to my research assistant, Deming E. Sherman, for services far in excess of the normal demands of such a job; and to Professor Ambrose Saricks of the University of Kansas, who was kind enough to read and criticize much of the manuscript.

J. G. Gagliardo, *Lawrence, Kansas*

Contents

1 / The Enlightenment

In its broadest signification, the Enlightenment in the forms it took in the eighteenth century refers to a stage of the long process of the secularization of Western thought since the Middle Ages. It may be regarded, in historical perspective, as a provisional culmination of attempts to provide a universally valid approach to the explanation of the world and of man in the world, for which the theological approach of the medieval mind, rooted in revelation and church tradition, had proved increasingly inadequate. The earlier splendid success of medieval theology in providing explanations of the medieval world had many causes; not least among them were the relative simplicity and uniformity of the world it purported to explain and the comparative lack of rapid change in that world.

But through the period we know as the Renaissance—a term often used merely as a convenient expression for three centuries or so of rapid change in almost every aspect of European society —the relative simplicity and uniformity of the medieval world were transformed into complexity and diversity at a pace that seemed always faster and more frantic. It is not our task to pursue these changes in detail; the briefest outline must suffice. Beginning in northern Italy and northwestern Europe and continuing to spread with very unequal rapidity to other parts of the continent, a process of economic differentiation began, providing a stimulus to profound alterations in the structure of political and social life. The number and size of urban centers increased; and their

1

growth—and that of the economic activities associated with them —not only led to the creation of increasingly more distinct and antagonistic social classes within the cities themselves but also introduced new competition between cities (or city-states) and produced a certain tension between urban areas and rural districts. Within cities, struggles between employers and employees over wages and other economic matters were joined by conflicts between wealthy patrician families for control of political power. The city-states of Italy vied for control of an expanding volume of trade, as did Central European towns. Urban areas, meanwhile, with their commercial orientation, were concerned with the commoditization of all goods, while rural districts, based on agriculture, were dependent for their social stability on the permanence of land values—i.e., on the non-commoditization of land; mutual distrust and resentment grew up between noble and peasant landowners, on one hand, and merchants and moneylenders of the towns, on the other hand, as well as between creditors and debtors, whether urban or rural.

All of these antagonisms created pressures that found frequent expression in conflicts of one kind or another—in the cities, strikes, riots, and revolutions, too frequent and widespread to catalogue; and in the countryside, peasant revolts, some of really serious proportions. These struggles reinforced in all strata of society an atmosphere of insecurity and fear, which many other (sometimes related) occurrences from the fourteenth to the sixteenth century had also contributed to produce. The great plagues of the mid-fourteenth century known collectively as the "Black Death"; the Hundred Years' War (1337–1453) between the ruling dynasties of England and France; the internal struggles between feudal monarchs and their vassals, tending always towards greater concentration of political authority in the hands of the former; and, in the late fifteenth century, the French invasion of Italy, beginning a protracted series of "modern" dynastic wars in Europe—these events all present the picture of violence, upheaval, and profound change that threw down the walls of the medieval order and altered permanently and drastically the objective conditions of European social life.

This terrible instability of life, greater than at any time since the ninth century, produced severe psychological dislocations among the people of western Europe, especially among the masses. It was natural that they should turn to their Church for comfort and solace, for this religious edifice had always explained the ways of God to man and, in doing so, had consoled him. In the thirteenth century, a considerable increase in the number of itinerant mendicant friars, preaching at the popular level, had seemed to represent the Church's recognition of the increased need for direct religious experience among the common folk. But it was not enough; and before long, the universal Church found itself beset by a series of controversies that seemed to threaten its claims to universality and to the guardianship of men's souls.

An increase in lay preaching in the fourteenth century, the appearance of messianic and chiliastic doctrines, and finally the bursting forth of two great new heretical movements in the late fourteenth century—those of the Lollards in England and the Hussites in Bohemia—posed a deepening challenge to church control of doctrine. At the same time, conflicts between the Church and the rising national monarchs, especially in France, over questions of church appointments and papal control of ecclesiastical administration led eventually, in the fourteenth century, to a long period of French "captivity" of the popes at Avignon and later to the spectacle of two, then three, popes, all claiming to be the legitimate head of the Church. This bitter struggle was ended, at least temporarily, in the early fifteenth century; but the numerous divisions of allegiance that had become evident in this long period of troubles continued to exist and formed part of the background for the great movements of the Reformation in the sixteenth century.

The Reformation itself, however it may have contributed to the breakdown of medieval Christian unity, was in many respects an attempt to salvage a theological world view in the face of the inadequacies of the old church, by bringing theological doctrines to bear on the great and disturbing issues of the time. For, in their first phases, the various strands of reformed thought—whether Lutheran, Calvinist, Anabaptist, or whatever—were characterized by a tremendous dynamism based on the abandonment of abstract theological metaphysics (scholasticism) and the adoption of a more practical and human approach to the concrete problems of the day. Later, of course, Protestantism was to develop its own dry dogmatics and become removed from day-to-day issues. And it was to fall victim to the same disease that originally had been responsible for its separation from orthodox Catholicism: sectarianism, a doctrinal and organizational proliferation of separatist groups that has continued to the present century.

In the elaboration of secular approaches to the understanding of the world, the foregoing is of great importance, for we can see in it not only the growth of a host of new conditions and events and problems requiring explanation and solution, but also the reasons why many men began to find it difficult to locate answers they sought within an exclusively Christian theological framework. The unity of medieval knowledge was no more; what was increasingly apparent, in fact, was that men were less and less able to agree even on that revealed truth that was supposed to be the very foundation of all knowledge. Under these circumstances, a growth of skepticism about religious explanations of the world was almost inevitable. But skepticism does not always take the form of open doubt, especially among men who do not know the meaning of the word. Religious doubt, in particular, is often expressed as inspiration towards a reformed religiosity, as in heretical movements and great religious renewals; and sometimes it appears as an intensified interest in non-religious matters or a loss of self-conscious concern with religious questions.

Long before the eighteenth-century English poet and philosopher Alexander Pope suggested that the proper study of mankind was man himself, the dictum was being acted upon by the humanist scholars of the early Renaissance. Their "rediscovery" of the literature of classical antiquity was significant not so much for the vast body of Latin and Greek prose that it provided for the delectation of grammarians, nor for the stylistic excellence that provided a model for the imitation of poetasters, but more for the novel ideas and secular emphases that flowed through it into the consciousness of an intellectual world, which was at precisely this moment open to receive new thoughts, new explanations, and a new idiom. It was a mature literature, filled with tolerance and humanity, with an interest in man and his works for their own sake, evincing a confidence in human reason, and expressive of a kind of objective relativity based on wide experience and wise judgment. To the influence of this stimulus toward augmented interest in man must be added the curiosity and excitement aroused by the age of geographical discoveries, which brought forth continually new evidences of the variety of human institutions, customs, and beliefs, and which challenged the imagination and the understanding of Europeans.

Furthermore, while the literature of the fifteenth and sixteenth centuries is full of a sense of foreboding and impending disaster, replete with the most terrifying prognostications of death, destruction, and damnation and with many jeremiads on the malice, impiety, and disloyalty of men—all a reaction to the turbulence and vicissitudes of these extraordinary times—there often occurs, side-by-side with these comments in the same works, a kind of awestruck wonder and a puerile boastfulness at the progress of the age and the excellence of man's recent achievements. Men proudly drew up lists of evidences of such progress in everything from printing and the invention of the compass to gunpowder, astronomy, literature, and the arts and bragged that their age was at least the equal of any that had ever been. The growth of these cultural riches was stimulated partly by a demand for elegance that had arisen among the well-to-do classes of the commercial cities of Europe, as well as among the expanding secular and ecclesiastical courts, whose patrons, like urban patricians, needed little instruction in the enjoyment of the secular conveniences and luxuries of a more affluent age.

While this age of change had therefore created totally new problems, it had also produced a creative response among the men who lived in it; and, though theology and religion were anything but forgotten by men whose lives still seemed so dependent on chance or fortune, their confidence in a good life achieved through reason based on experience of the world around them was gradually increasing—though perhaps not as yet very self-consciously. And it was beginning to contradict the earlier theological insistence on man as a creature doomed to unremitting toil and unrelieved suffering on this earth by the fact of original sin and its resultant human depravity. An increasing tendency toward the more efficient organization of human enterprise, whether of the state (as manifest in the development of law and bureaucracy) or of private business (seen in the elaboration of a whole host of commercial techniques and practices), not only demonstrates an increased amount of rational planning, but also created a greater need for men trained as experts in secular pursuits, especially law.

This expanding secular base of European thought brought with it a gradual insistence on the principle of tolerance. Tolerance itself has been often associated historically with the phenomenon of urbanism—largely because the city has depended on commerce for its livelihood, and because commerce usually involves an exposure to strangers and foreigners and the necessity of tolerating their personal and ideological peculiarities in order to do business with them. The humanistic works of the sixteenth century, which were the products not only of classical scholarship but of an urban environment as well, were some of the first to put forward both logical and charitable reasons for religious tolerance. More compelling arguments came gradually over the course of the sixteenth and seventeenth centuries, the period of the great religious wars in France and Germany and of related struggles in other states. By the end of these bitter civil conflicts—the late sixteenth century in France, the mid-seventeenth in Germany—exhaustion and stalemate themselves had produced the concept of tolerance as a political necessity.

The hardheaded yet supple theorists of the new dynastic and territorial sovereigns had some success in convincing their equally hardheaded masters, the princes who ruled these strife-ridden states, that the foundations of civil power—economic prosperity and social unity—made the luxury of indulgence in confessional wars indefensibly expensive. In some states, therefore, a very limited sort of tolerance was introduced; hedged by numerous restrictions for the minority faith, tolerance often guaranteed little more than one's right to one's own conscience without fear of being slaughtered for it. Seldom did it confer full civic equality or even the right to public worship. Even in this limited sense, formal tolerance lasted not a full hundred years in France, and was revoked by Louis XIV in 1685. In other places where it had existed, it continued a rather precarious existence throughout the eighteenth century, not without occasional lapses.

But to the leaders of the more worldly oriented streams of thought, toleration had become an intellectual as well as a political necessity. As a political phenomenon, tolerance suggests merely the necessity of accommodation to diversity of opinion in order to maintain peace; as an intellectual phenomenon, it is rooted in the insight that truth itself is the result of a search that must entail diverse opinion—that freedom of expression is an indispensable means toward the discovery of truth. This insight was not easily won, for it was frankly difficult for men to understand how the unity of civil society—i.e., peace—could be maintained without unity of belief; it is a difficulty not peculiar to early modern Europe. But for men to have attained this kind of understanding of tolerance, it was necessary for them, first, to have rejected the notion that divine revelation was itself adequate to explain everything in the world, and second, to have accepted the possibility of attaining knowledge of the world by some other means. We have seen the process whereby the first of these came about among a number of educated men; it remains for us to explore the second.

The intellectual confidence that seems to be such a fundamental characteristic of the secular philosophers of the eighteenth century reduces in large measure to their conviction that they had developed a foolproof *method* for discovering truth. They had, they said, finally hit upon an approach to the correct understanding of the world that would not only depict the world accurately, but in doing so also would outfit mankind with the general principles of true rules of thought and behavior. This method was due partly to the work and influence of specific figures of the intellectually fertile seventeenth century, and partly to a consensus derived from literally hundreds of major and minor essayists, astronomers, physicians, legal scholars, and other progressive spirits from the sixteenth century onwards. The discoveries of astronomers such as Copernicus, Kepler, Galileo, and others were especially impressive throughout this period—not just because of their conclusions, which led to the gradual acceptance of the heliocentric universe, but also because of their demonstration that man, with his own abilities, could discover and formulate knowledge about his world.

In the early seventeenth century, Francis Bacon, philosopher and English government official, attempted to sketch out part of an outline for a whole new revival of knowledge, called the *Novum Organum*, in which the rejection of traditional systems of knowledge and the reliance on specific sense data formed the basis for a new method designed to give man knowledge of—and therefore the ability to operate effectively in—the world around him. At about the same time, the French mathematician Réné Descartes, searching for "a universal mathematics that would explain all," elaborated a series of methodological principles that included systematic doubt, logical analysis, the strict progression of synthesis, careful review of procedures and conclusions, and, finally, the attempt to assert mathematics as a language of universal precision. While Bacon and Descartes were in complete disagreement on some basic points, their common rejection of traditional authority and their common emphasis on the importance of method, when combined with eclectic syntheses of their thought by others, produced a mental revolution that was symbolized, even for his own contemporaries, by the gigantic figure of Isaac Newton (1642–1727).

Newton's significance in the history of Western thought lies perhaps less in his specialized work on optics, light, gravitation, and mathematics, important though it was, than in the grand synthesis he drew of the physical order of the universe and in the mathematical demonstration of the validity of this synthesis. His *Mathematical Principles of Natural Philosophy*, first published in Latin in 1687, appeared to provide conclusive proof that the physical universe, in its entirety, operated according to fixed and definite laws—Natural laws—and that these laws could be discovered and accurately known. Here, then, was Nature, a great mechanical work of God, which could be known directly without the intervention and intermediation of theological or other traditional philosophical authorities.

It was not long before the implication was drawn that God had provided in the laws of Nature a surer guide for proper human action than in revelation, whose actual meaning appeared so difficult for men to agree upon. As early as 1615, Galileo had suggested that human scientific experience manifested a much greater degree of common agreement than did the interpretation of revelation among squabbling theologians, and that science itself—i.e., the observation of physical phenomena—might be employed to assist in the explanation of scripture, especially in cases where literal interpretations contradicted ordinary experience and common sense. Now, after Newton, it was possible to go still further, and to assert that God had placed His commands in the laws of Nature themselves, and that the knowledge of those laws would give man the principles of his own right action. Man and his society were but a part of the universal order of Nature; by bringing himself, his laws, and his institutions into harmony with the laws of Nature, man might thereby assure himself of a better life.

But it still remained to be demonstrated that man had the ability to do this. Traditional theological interpretations of the nature of man held that through original sin man had become innately depraved, tending always towards sin and incapable of discovering truth except when guided by God's grace through revelation. This notion had to a considerable extent been discarded, if only implicitly, by successive generations of increasingly secularized philosophers and scientists since the Renaissance, whose own work is a monument to their already great confidence in human reason. But it was left to another Englishman, John Locke (1632–1704), to provide a formal and analytical basis for the positive powers of human reason, and thus to make belief in reason and the human mind a self-conscious and active force. Locke's *Essay Concerning Human Understanding* (1690) showed that man's ideas were all a result of sense impressions from the external world and of the subsequent operation of his mind on the consciousness created by those impressions. Locke thus asserted that every man had by nature the physical faculties to receive experiences, to remember and compare them, and in this way to adjust his thoughts and actions to a standard of truth that Newton and his numerous popularizers had meanwhile showed to reside in the laws of Nature. Thus, while man was a product of his environment, he could also change his environment to conform with the laws of Nature through the exercise of his reason.

Locke and Newton did not create the eighteenth-century Enlightenment; what they did do was to provide a convenient set of categories and a framework where a number of issues and attitudes that had been growing more strongly into the consciousness of educated Europeans for literally hundreds of years could find a home. The immense popularity that their teachings achieved almost instantly, in their vulgarized forms, can be explained only by the degree to which they filled a widely felt need for a terminology and a more or less complete system of principles for clothing a group of vague and imprecise dissatisfactions and hopes. The concepts of Reason and Nature play a vastly important role in eighteenth-century thought; but this stems at least partly from their appropriateness as vehicles for carrying the strongly held and simple conviction that man could discover truth, increase knowledge, and use that knowledge to improve his situation in the world.

For our purposes, it is the attitudes towards society and government developed as ramifications of this conviction that are of primary importance. It is difficult to make brief generalizations about the immense variety of attitudes expressed by the literally thousands of popular philosophers of the eighteenth century who tried to suggest means of improving human society through the utilization of the key concepts of Reason and Nature. Their disagreements among themselves, their own instinctive distrust of "system-building," and their tendency to jump from one subject to another after only superficial exploration, all combine to make easy categorization impossible. More than any other single object of their attention, however, it is probably the realm of moral philosophy that lay at the center of the *philosophes'* views on man, society, and politics. Morality, in its broadest sense, pertains to the science and practice of right conduct; and, as the *philosophes* knew from the outset, once the proper bases of right conduct were known, it should then—but only then—be possible to determine what social institutions might best stimulate and accommodate right conduct.

The traditional moral norms propounded by the various

Christian denominations had already been rejected definitely by most of the *philosophes*, who regarded the revelation on which they were founded as a superstition that utterly failed to measure up to their standards of rational criticism. Many *philosophes* had in fact altered their own religious beliefs and had come to adopt one or another form of "natural religion," as it was usually called. Deism, one such form, rejected the concept of a personal and omnipresent God entirely and maintained that God, having created the universe to operate according to fixed and eternal laws, had thereafter withdrawn from it, leaving it entirely self-sufficient, like a perpetual clock. Another closely related belief, pantheism, tended to see the spirit of God merely as the sum total of the laws and forces of Nature herself.

These new creeds provide evidence of the increasing conviction that the universe was self-sufficient, and that Nature could provide all of the knowledge necessary to man for the construction of his own life. In the area of moral ideas, the seventeenth century had once again indicated something of the direction that the eighteenth century was to take. Thomas Hobbes (1588–1679), an English political theorist, had written a secular defense of absolute monarchy based on the premise that man, a creature of Nature, was motivated in all his actions by the instinct of self-preservation. Hobbes then went on to derive not merely society and government, but a specific form of government—monocratic authoritarianism—from this instinct. This, together with man's innate capacity to reason out the means whereby instinct might best be satisfied, defined the nature of man.

The popular philosophers of the eighteenth century, especially in France, accepted certain parts of the Hobbesian argument, though in modified form. First, they accepted the notion that man's nature could be defined only by his conduct—i.e., that a knowledge of human nature, like the nature of the universe, could come only from an observation of behavior. Second, they accepted instincts, inborn drives, together with the ability to reason, as the irreducible kernel of human nature; and third, they accepted self-preservation, but tended to see it as only one part of a larger human drive, the pursuit of happiness in general. It was the instinct of every individual to achieve happiness, which was operationally defined as the courting of pleasure and the avoidance of pain. The mainspring of human action therefore came to be regarded in terms of self-love, or self-interest (*amour propre*)—a principle that the eighteenth century never ceased to praise itself for discovering. And it was fully in character that the "moral scientists" who discovered the principle of self-interest—for that was how the *philosophes* conceived of themselves—should regard it as neither good nor bad, but merely so; after all, the nature of man, again like the nature of the universe, was a fact, not a judgment.

What followed from all this, for the *philosophes,* was that human law, society, and government were not the creations of God, but rather the consequences of human reason in its pursuit of happiness; as the Baron de Montesquieu, an early *philosophe,* put it in his *Spirit of the Laws* (1748): "Law in general is human reason, inasmuch as it governs all the inhabitants of the earth." The same was held to be true of all social institutions, whose origin could ultimately be traced to the attempts of human reason to satisfy human needs and wants. From here, it was but a step to the assertion that the institutions of human society received justification for existence only from their utility as rational means to preserve and increase human happiness.

There were certain difficulties in this general approach, however. One of the most obvious was the problem of explaining how millions of individuals, living together in society, could all pursue their individual self-interest without continual conflicts with other individuals doing the same thing, thus producing an eternal state of chaos. The answer came in the acceptance of one or another form of the social contract theory, according to which, men in a primitive "state of nature" agreed to form a civil body, or society, and to submit to a set of laws that would be common to them all. Whether the motive was fear of mutual extinction, as Hobbes had written in *Leviathan* (1651), or the desire to guarantee more efficiently the mutual observance of natural rights such as life, liberty, and property, as Locke had said in his *Of Civil Government* (1690), or, finally, the wish to improve by collective action the conditions of life of every individual, as Jean-Jacques Rousseau suggested in the *Social Contract* (1762), eighteenth-century theorists were agreed that a social contract was entered into as a means for providing common standards whereby social life could be carried on to the benefit of the individuals composing it.

It is quite true that some significant differences showed up in the *philosophes'* conceptions of the actual bases of cooperation: Rousseau and his followers in France, along with the majority of British moralists, tended to believe that an instinctive and innate sympathy toward his fellow man existed in every individual, who was thus inclined by nature to help and cooperate with others; while the main body of French thinkers (Voltaire, Condillac, Helvétius, and many others) asserted that cooperation was really nothing more or less than a complex series of interlocked mutual exploitations, based on individual selfishness, whose overall effect, however, was socially beneficial and progressive. Again, however, all were agreed that whether law and government were established to facilitate and implement positive cooperation or merely to set necessary and agreed-upon limitations to individual competition, their character and preservation ought to rest on the criterion of their contribution to human happiness.

A second problem of this approach arose with the necessity of reconciling the axiomatic uniformity of human nature everywhere in the world with what was quite obviously *not* a uniformity of laws, customs, beliefs, and governmental forms throughout the world. How was one to explain this apparent contradiction? Montesquieu in his *Spirit of the Laws* gave the answer that was most widely accepted and used for nearly one hundred years: While the nature of man was everywhere the same, said he, the physical environments where men lived were different. Climate, geography, the nature and quality of the soil, and even habit and custom created specific needs in some places that did not exist in others and sometimes made it necessary to satisfy even the same needs in different ways; this had led to the creation of different laws and institutions as instruments of solving human problems.

By a sometimes rather questionable and perfunctory survey of contemporary travel literature and ancient classical texts, Montesquieu thus hoped to show that, underneath the bewildering diversity of social organizations that existed in the world, there was a basic similarity which consisted in the appropriateness of institutions, under the circumstances given by Nature, as means of supplying an essentially common set of human needs. He also tried to develop generalizations about the kind of laws and institutions that might best serve men in various kinds of environments, thus reflecting a common belief among the *philosophes*—in spite of their admission of the possibility that several means might adequately serve the same end—that there was, at least in theory, a single best institution to accomplish a given purpose in a given situation. Montesquieu's work represented a kind of primitive sociology, which helped to produce a profound difference in the ways Europeans looked at themselves and at other peoples in the world. It gave them a deeper insight into the reasons for human diversity, increased their tolerance for differences, and also strengthened the belief in the ability of reason to match solutions to problems.

But here, of course, was a third difficulty. If, indeed, the social world was a creation of man's reason designed to provide solutions to his problems and thus to increase the sum of human happiness, then how was it possible to explain the continued existence of so much misery and unhappiness in the world? The answer to this question, and one that opened a channel for torrents of criticism of European society, was that ignorance and fraud, trading on one another, had in the past created institutions and beliefs that were at best inapplicable and at worst directly inimical to a happy and harmonious life for all. Almost none of the *philosophes* denied that mankind, in its long history, had made strides towards happiness or maintained that progress was uniquely bound to their own age. But they were convinced that such progress as had occurred had been slow, halting, and in many instances almost accidental. They knew only too well that human reason could err and be misled; and even in their own time, there was among them a certain streak of pessimism, based on their own experience and their knowledge of history, which tempered somewhat the generally optimistic forecasts of a rapid improvement of man's condition. Still, they now had a method of discovering truth and a heightened self-consciousness of man's ability to make use of it that would guarantee greater progress if only their ideas could achieve the necessary currency in society.

From the viewpoint of the *philosophes,* revealed religion in general, Christianity in particular, and especially the Catholic church, were not only the primary obstacle to the propagation of their new teachings in their own time, but had throughout history performed an essentially obscurantist function. The priestly class, whether out of lunacy, mistaken zeal, or desire to feather its own nest, had traded on man's hopes, fears, and ignorance in such a way as to hinder the progress of the human mind, and to make of itself an intellectual authoritarian caste with many vested social, economic, and political interests. In France, the center of the eighteenth-century enlightenment, the Catholic church had wide powers of censorship, either directly or through influence on other corporations and groups that had such powers; and it used its position to oppose vigorously the introduction of the ideas of the *philosophes,* which of course denied the foundations on which its authority—social as well as intellectual—rested. Because of the key position of the Church, it was therefore entirely natural that the most bitter and consistent criticism of the *philosophes* throughout the century was directed against the Church.

No one was more dedicated to the destruction of ecclesiastical authority than the famous Voltaire, who tried to carry out his own motto, "Écrasez l'infame!" ("Crush the infamous thing!"), in literally hundreds of writings of various kinds over a long career. Satire was the favorite literary instrument of Voltaire, as of many of his fellows, who heaped scorn on the immoral lives of clergymen, on blind fanaticism, on the irrationality of the Christian faith, on the inconsistency of Biblical texts, and so on. Some of the *philosophes* tried to demonstrate that the kernel of all the great religions of the world reduced to a few simple ethical principles, which could just as well have been derived from the laws of Nature, and without the useless and expensive ceremonies, rituals, dogmas, and priesthoods that had made organized religion burdensome to mankind. Still others attacked the political influence of the Church and attempted to explore and expose what they saw as the insidious influences exercised by the Church on various aspects of social life. Above all, though, religious and intellectual tolerance was the cry; and the Church, standing squarely astride the path of free thought as interpreted by the *philosophes*, was therefore first, last, and always their most implacable enemy. It should be pointed out, however, that the violently anti-clerical tone of the French *philosophes* was generally much less marked among their counterparts in Protestant countries and in other Catholic lands.

The numerous criticisms of other aspects of eighteenth-century society in which the *philosophes* indulged cannot be listed here in any detail. At base, most of them were derived from the self-conscious attempt to subject all the features of public life, and not a few of private life, to a rational scrutiny, in which the standard of acceptability was the degree that the object of attention was calculated to preserve or increase the sum of human happiness. Institutions, ideas, or practices that did not meet this standard, whether because they were malicious or useless or irrationally established, were attacked in books, periodicals, and pamphlets with means that ranged from acid humor to thunderous denunciation. They criticized governmental inefficiency, corruption, and waste; warfare and concomitant aristocratic ideals of military glory; the stupidity and unnecessary harshness of the laws and their unequal application; arbitrary and harmful restrictions on the freedom of movement of individuals and goods; and a host of lesser abuses and social irrationalities that tended to impede the achievement of the proper goal of social organization—the improvement of man's life.

While it is true that many of these criticisms contained within themselves suggestions for the corrections of the abuses they attacked, it is also true that the *philosophes* had no real "program" in the sense of any comprehensive set of final reform goals. It has often been remarked that the *philosophes* were reformers, concerned with the betterment of the society they lived in, not revolutionaries, dedicated to its destruction. The accuracy of this judgment is generally borne out not only by the lack of systematic attention to large-scale reform projects, but also by the relative unimportance of political questions in their works. Most of the *philosophes* accepted some version of the social contract theory, according to which, government originated by an agreement of the governed and derived its powers from them. And most would have agreed with Locke that the purpose of this government was to protect certain rights of the people who had founded it. But the question of how this was to be done, in a constitutional sense, did not occupy a very prominent place in their thoughts; and, if only for lack of anything better, they tended to settle for the existing political forms.

This tendency can be illustrated by the proposals of one group of French *philosophes,* the *Économistes,* or, as they have since come to be known, the Physiocrats. Their work, from the late 1750's onwards, represented an attempt to apply the laws of Nature to economic affairs and to suggest changes in economic systems implied by the results of their investigations. From the natural right of self-preservation, they derived property—private property—as a necesary instrument, and then concluded that the right of private property necessarily included the right to manipulate that property freely to one's own advantage—i.e., to buy and sell in a free market. The Physiocrats further believed that only the extractive industries—agriculture, fishing, mining, forestry, etc.—could produce a real or "pure" product and thus increase wealth; for industry merely changed the form of "pure" (raw) produce, and commerce only transported it from one place to another. The implication of these ideas was that all proprietary and commercial relationships should be as free as possible, with emphasis on freedom of the grain trade, which would do much to raise the economic position of agriculture and, in combination with the cessation of artificial government support of various branches of industry and commerce, would produce a more balanced and progressive economic system.

In view of prevailing mercantilist and protectionist policies of European states, these proposals can be termed almost revolutionary, since free exchange implied not only a shift in domestic economic policies, but also an abandonment of the long-standing international commercial hostility so typical of seventeenth- and eighteenth-century Europe. But the Physiocrats who dealt with the problem of how their reforms might actually be implemented generally saw no need for any fundamental alteration in the monarchical government that then existed. In fact, most of them believed that only a single absolute authority, a monarch, could claim the amount of authority necessary to cut through the maze of corporate privileges, vested interests, and irrational economic principles that would have to be abolished if their new system were to be established. Thus, some of them spoke of the benefits of a "legal despotism," i.e., absolute sovereign authority acting without the exterior restraint of selfish groups, but under the self-imposed control of enlightened legal principles derived from the infallible Nature herself.

Alexander Pope, in his *Essay on Man* (1733), expressed well the general indifference of most enlightened reformers to basic political questions when he wrote:

> For forms of government let fools contest;
> Whate'er is best administer'd is best.

Yet it is possible to locate three broad currents of thought on constitutional forms among the variety of rather confused notions that occurred here and there in the *philosophes'* writings. For the first, we may take the opinions of Voltaire as representative. Professor Peter Gay has called Voltaire's position one of "constitutional absolutism," and as such it was far and away the most commonly held of the three. Stripped to essentials, it was a position founded on a lack of realistic alternatives to monarchical absolutism—in view of the selfishness of the aristocracy and the ignorance of the masses—combined with a belief in the ability of monarchy to govern well as long as it was restricted by some guarantees of individual rights, and especially if it were enlightened by philosophy. While opinions about where such restrictions ought to come from differed, public opinion and self-restraint based on the traditional—i.e., unwritten—constitution of the country were frequently mentioned.

A second position, advocated most cogently by Montesquieu, himself a nobleman, was that of an aristocratic monarchy, in which royal power would be subject to fairly concrete checks by the nobility—regarded as a political corporation—and in which the chief guarantees against tyranny would consist in granting some share of both legislative and executive (administrative) authority to members of the nobility, individually and in groups. This view was rejected by many *philosophes* precisely because it would confer more political power on a group that, in their opinion, was second only to the clergy in its opposition to progressive reform. The third, and in this period the weakest, of the main directions of political thought, was represented by Rousseau in his *Social Contract*. Searching for a formula that would reconcile completely the freedom of the individual with the imperatives of social organization, Rousseau developed the doctrines of popular sovereignty and political democracy, by which government became merely the administrative organ of the general will of the people, utterly subject to its control. Thoroughly radical for the time, it exercised comparatively little influence until after the great Revolution had begun.

Finally, then, the *philosophes* must be regarded as a small, if growing, body of popular essayists, philosophers, and reformers who asked for a variety of changes in society, whose implications and total effect would be revolutionary only in the sense that they would signalize a new, enlightened, or rational approach to human social problems. For the rest, the *philosophes* accepted a very large part of the societies they lived in. And, for all their oft-repeated protestations to the contrary, they were also accepted or at least tolerated by a large and influential part of their society. It is true of course that their ideas were opposed by many and were unknown to many more; but educated Europe knew them increasingly well as the eighteenth century wore on, and informed men of the middle classes, among the aristocracy, and on·the thrones of the various states of the continent did not find them universally unpalatable.

It is no accident that the *philosophes* were not always seen as the *enfants terribles* that they sometimes took themselves to be; for, while they were the first to speak of themselves as "enlightened" and the first to use the terms *éclaircissement* and *Aufklärung* as descriptions of their age, their place had long been prepared for them. The flower has many stages of growth, of which the blooming is only one; and so it was with the eighteenth century, which was really only one of the stages of "The Enlightenment." As this entire chapter should indicate, the seeds of this enlightenment were sown centuries before Montesquieu penned his first Persian letter, or Voltaire had his first encounter at the baptismal font with the Infamous Thing. A greater interest in the things of this world, a greater confidence in man and his works and his reason, the growing appetite of curiosity and the growing restlessness of the unsatisfied mind—all these things form less a doctrine than a spirit. And it would be well to remember, in the sequel, that it was a spirit that, from its beginnings, could always animate princes as well as philosophers.

2 / Monarchs and Reform

The monarchs who governed the European states after the middle of the eighteenth century were characterized by a certain similarity of personal culture that made them, as a group, rather sharply distinct even from their immediate predecessors. They constituted the first generation of princes to have been brought up and educated in the full flowering of the artistic movements of the Rococo and the literary publicists of the Enlightenment. The courts where they grew to manhood and rulership in many cases already reflected much of the secularism, wit, and cultural cosmopolitanism that were so much the earmarks of the polite intellectual world of the *salons* and the *philosophes* of the eighteenth century. In other cases, though their environments may have remained rude and parochial, princes took to themselves tutors, advisors, and friends who had an interest in the world of art, literature, and philosophy and who provided them with an oasis of culture where their own interest could grow to at least a superficial permanence.

So general did at least a passing acquaintanceship with the leading intellectual and artistic movements of the time become among them that it began to appear almost a necessary adjunct to rulership that princes be conversant with—and even to an extent leaders of—the refined world of high culture. The profundity of their understanding of the major works of intellect of their time was not always very great, perhaps, but a few of them actually made personal contributions of some value to literature and the arts. Frederick II of Prussia, for example, whose cultured tastes and interests were won at considerable emotional expense to himself at the harsh and disciplined court of his somewhat boorish father, wrote political philosophy, poetry, and music, of which some is still considered fairly respectable. Other major rulers, such as Catherine II of Russia, Joseph II of Austria, Leopold of Tuscany and Austria, Charles III of Spain, Gustavus III of Sweden, and a host of lesser princes and statesmen, read widely in the works of the *philosophes* and conducted court cultures that were more than mere gestures towards the appearance of refinement.

Above all, the differences between the atmosphere and energy of these courts and their counterparts of one or two generations earlier is very striking. The widespread disinterest in, and occasional contempt for, intellectualism, often unrelieved even by patronizing attitudes that characterized many courts of the late seventeenth and early eighteenth centuries, was closely tied to the dominance of an aristocratic ideal of merit that included birth, military valor, and a high life-style involving hunting, gambling, and riotous entertainment, but leaving books, science, and art to men of lesser origins. The courts of the late eighteenth century, however, and their royal leadership show evidence of a growing contempt for the aristocratic ignoramuses of yesteryear and a desire to emulate and surround themselves with the cultural sophistication of the new class of semi-professional intellectuals whom we know as the *philosophes.*

Not least among the factors that established a community of interest between "enlightenment" and "despotism" was the self-conscious adoption by monarchs of a new standard of values that propelled the role and discussion of ideas into a prominent place in court life. This did not, of course, efface older values completely; but it created a new and direct liaison between power and philosophy, further strengthened by the eagerness of monarchs to entertain leading *philosophes* at their courts—Berlin, St. Petersburg, Florence, and so on—for varying lengths of time. The most obvious origins of "enlightened despotism" lie, therefore, in the education, tastes, and interests of a whole generation of princes whose patronage of intellect created an impression of novelty that was as noteworthy to contemporaries as it has been to historians since.

But the extent to which their work reflected their great personal preoccupation with philosophic ideas is another question —and a very difficult one. It can be answered only by looking at their activity as heads of state in the context of the goals and motivations of their reforms. In the following description of reforms undertaken during the period in question and in their evaluation, it will become obvious that the analytical categories established are not entirely exclusive of one another; this, of course, is due to the inevitable failure of any scheme of analysis to encompass fully the unity of simultaneous events. Cross references will be made, however, to indicate, where necessary, that a given reform must be regarded as significant in more than one categorical context.

GOVERNMENTAL AND ADMINISTRATIVE REFORM

We may conveniently begin discussion of the reform work of this period with the alterations and innovations brought to the structure of government and administrative systems; the division by states that appears here will not be followed in other categories, but is almost essential in this case because of the great diversity of inherited political institutions in the different countries.

Austria

By 1765, when the Empress Maria Theresa accepted her son Joseph II as co-regent of the Austrian hereditary lands, she had already accomplished several important governmental reforms in her quarter-century of lone rule. Reacting vigorously to the nearly disastrous outcome of the War of the Austrian Succession and aided by capable advisors such as Kaunitz, Haugwitz, and Chotek, Maria Theresa in the late 1740's undertook a large-scale reorganization of the central administration in Vienna, designed primarily to improve the administration of finances and the military establishment by defining the competence of various offices more clearly and eliminating overlapping functions. This reorganization was capped in 1760 by the creation of a State Council (*Staatsrat*) of advisors that acted as a coordinating control organ between the monarch and the actual administrative departments.

The Empress and her advisors also recognized the great need for provincial and local reform; but because her dominions included such widely different areas as the Austrian Netherlands, Hungary, and parts of northern Italy as well as the central German and Bohemian territories, all of which had traditional administrative organs whose members were extremely jealous of their positions, they wisely decided to concentrate for the time being only on the Austrian (German) and Bohemian lands of the Crown, which for some time had been subject to greater control by the Crown, and which were regarded as forming the most dependable "kernel" area of the monarchy. In each of the provinces of Austria and Bohemia, an administrative board or college was established, and in each district of each province, a District Officer with a staff of subordinate officials. A parent body in Vienna supervised the activities of these provincial and local officers, whose functions were slowly expanded after 1750 to include supervision of military recruitment, financing, and supply, as well as of agrarian relationships and general economic affairs.

When Joseph became sole ruler upon the death of his mother in 1780, he not only intensified central control of this kernel area, but attempted also to impose on the peripheral areas of the monarchy—the Austrian Netherlands, Hungary, and Lombardy— a single integrated administration that would allow the Crown for the first time to regard all its possessions as a unitary state. In Austria and Bohemia, he sharply increased the scope of functions of royal officers, created new administrative districts, and required municipal officials to be certified by the central government. In Bohemia, he changed the traditional constitution, overrode protests of the noble estates and the municipalities, and ceased to consult them altogether. He removed the Crown of St. Stephen, symbol of his authority in Hungary, to Vienna, and in numerous ways began assaults on traditional privileges and on the semi-autonomy of Hungarian governmental agencies.

At the same time, he stepped up measures begun by Maria Theresa to whittle down the independence of the Lombard administration, which was largely in the hands of a Milanese patrician oligarchy, and eventually suppressed the Lombard senate entirely, thus turning the government of this Italian territory completely over to Austrian administration. Similar attacks were made on the autonomous administration of the Austrian Netherlands, leading to the suppression of many old offices and the introduction of new officials and new methods. Throughout the entire administration, Joseph tried to inspire a spirit of hard work, discipline, and duty, for which he himself set the example; but he left as little to chance as possible, and reinforced his work ethic by a system of administrative espionage.

By the late 1780's, Joseph had concentrated in his hands political power more absolute than had been possessed by any Austrian ruler before him. But the price of this extremely rapid accrual of power was that it remained impermanent. Serious revolts broke out in the Netherlands, Hungary, and Lombardy, and dissatisfaction in Austria and Bohemia approached a boiling point. Joseph began to recognize the seriousness of his situation only in his last illness; he called back many of his administrative and judicial reforms in Hungary, promised to return the Crown of St. Stephen, and then died, a bitter man, convinced that his rule had been a failure.

It was given to his brother Leopold II, who had watched Joseph's furious decade of reform from Tuscany with many misgivings, to preside over the revocation of many of Joseph's innovations, especially in the non-German areas of the monarchy. Leopold had a fertile mind, at once more supple and cautious than Joseph's, and would very likely have instituted a number of major reforms himself had he lived longer. But since he died only two years after Joseph, in 1792, and since he was too preoccupied with preventing rebellion in Austria and with winning back the Netherlands and Hungary to engage in innovation, he has been assigned the sad distinction of being the Emperor who merely negated much of Joseph's reform. As far as government and administrative organization is concerned, he above all returned many of the traditional privileges previously enjoyed by various areas of the monarchy, perhaps in the hope of constructing in the future a truly representative constitution for the entire monarchy.

Tuscany

The brevity of Leopold's reign in Austria is all the more tragic because of the reputation he had established as an enlightened ruler in the Grand Duchy of Tuscany from 1765 to 1790. In these years, Tuscany enjoyed a mild and progressive government, the result of Leopold's devotion to the welfare of the state. By assuring high officials of their posts during good behavior, he did much to end the enervating court intrigues and factions that had earlier tended to render government policies chaotic. He reformed municipal administration in the 1770's, creating a host of new and more responsible institutions, but at the same time provided for a really effective self-government involving representatives of all classes to make decisions relating to communal taxes, a budget, public works, and so on.

Leopold was convinced of the desirability of citizen participation in public life, chiefly because as a reformer he was dubious of the permanence and effectiveness of innovations that were not understood by those whom they were intended to benefit. Experience gained by citizens through involvement in public affairs would serve to educate them about government itself and would make Leopold's own reform work less difficult. To this end, in addition to the municipal reform, he created citizens' militias all over Tuscany in 1780–81 and, in 1782, capped all his governmental proposals with a great constitution—which unfortunately was never put into effect. It provided not only for a system of local, provincial, and national legislative assemblies with unheard-of powers in a monarchical state, but also imposed a number of important limitations on the power of the ruler. Interference in all civil jurisprudence was forbidden; revenues of the state and of the person of the ruler were to be strictly separate, and an accounting of the former was to be given to the representative assembly; no increase in armed forces, change in the militia system, or construction of fortresses, even with his personal funds, could be undertaken by the ruler; and so on.

This constitutional proposal, for which the constitutions of several of the new United States of America had provided identifiable hints, was never put into operation. Massive indifference among the citizenry, opposition from privileged groups, a threatening international situation, and Leopold's awareness of Emperor Joseph's decision to incorporate Tuscany into the Austrian administrative framework upon the death of either of the two brothers—all led to postponement and, ultimately, to the abandonment of the scheme. But in spite of this and the general lack of success of the militias, Leopold's administrative reorganizations and his improved bureaucracy gave Tuscany better government than it had ever enjoyed.

Prussia

The formal changes in the apparatus of government that Frederick II inherited in 1740 from his father, Frederick William I, were very few. The chief administrative body at the central level of the kingdom was the so-called General Directory, a board divided into departments whose business was apportioned among them according to both topical and geographical criteria. Functionally comparable subordinate agencies, the War- and Domains-Chambers, existed in each of the provinces. Frederick William I had already set the pattern for the position of the king in this arrangement; he ruled "from his cabinet," i.e., from his private office. There he received written reports and advice from the members of the General Directory and other agencies and, assisted by clerk-secretaries, then issued cabinet orders on paper to his administrative agencies, which implemented them down through the various levels of the bureaucracy.

Frederick II intensified this development towards highly personal "cabinet rule" and seldom asked for more than information—i.e., not even advice—from his administrators. He was greatly concerned that royal power not be diluted by excessive reliance on the royal bureaucracy; and thus, in addition to maintaining a system of royal administrative spies, he tended more or less deliberately to disorganize and decentralize the bureaucratic machine. For example, he created new departments and ministries whose heads corresponded with him directly or reported to him in person, rather than through the medium of the General Directory; he increasingly dealt with personalities rather than with collective boards; and he charged the administration of the province of Silesia, conquered from Austria in the 1740's, not to the General Directory, but to a special group of individuals under his immediate and personal supervision. Furthermore, he encouraged a limited revival of non-bureaucratic agencies of local corporate self-government among the rural nobility. All this was done to be sure that only the king himself would provide the cohesion necessary to the government of the country. Far from encouraging bureaucratic centralization, therefore, Frederick began to decentralize it, to the end of increasing his personal control. He interfered everywhere in the administration, and made himself, in fact as well as in theory, the most absolute ruler of all European states.

Russia

Catherine II, who came to the throne in 1762 after disposing of her imbecilic husband Peter III, was faced with the traditional problem of how to govern the vast, sprawling Russian Empire with a relatively small and badly trained bureaucracy. For Russia, real centralization was not actually a choice: the central government in St. Petersburg was not an especially inefficient one, perhaps, but the implementation of imperial command throughout the whole empire at provincial and local levels was a problem of staggering proportions. Realistically assessing her own position and the character of the country she ruled, Catherine decided early that the Russian landowning class, the gentry or nobility, held the real key to political power, and she decided to base her own autocratic authority on this class. This was done in several ways, but the one of greatest importance was the transformation of the gentry into unsalaried servants of the Crown.

The Russian gentry, unlike the nobility of other European countries, did not possess traditional corporate rights, with respect either to political organization or to social and economic security. Their titles and lands were utterly dependent on the Crown. Now, by extending and formally confirming specific privileges to this class, Catherine hoped to gain their allegiance and active cooperation in the work of governmental administration. A reorganization of local and provincial government in 1775 provided for a series of new administrative districts involving the participation of local gentry. Municipalities were also reorganized, and charters issued that attempted to imitate those of western European towns. The Crown also extended and legalized the patrimonial jurisdiction of the gentry over their peasants. Finally, in 1785, Catherine issued a Charter of the Nobility, which guaranteed the security, titles, and status of the Russian gentry according to several classes or ranks.

Throughout her reign, the Empress sought to establish a community of interest between the nobility and the Crown. In 1767, she convoked a kind of national representative assembly to work out a code of positive laws for the Empire—supposedly to be based on natural law. The work of this assembly ultimately came to nothing, but its mere existence exemplifies Catherine's desire to establish and maintain a cooperative understanding with the gentry, without whose help her own autocracy would have been ineffective. As a result of her work, she not only freed the Crown of a potential threat from the nobility at the beginning of her reign, but also made the imperial authority more real.

Spain

Since 1700, when the Crown of Spain had passed into the hands of a Bourbon dynasty, numerous efforts had been undertaken towards the centralization of the antiquated governing structure of an increasingly decrepit country. Special political laws (*fueros*) that granted a degree of autonomy to various provinces were abolished early in the century by Philip V, thus bringing all provinces into closer subjection to the central government in Madrid. A system of provincial commissariats, or intendancies, modelled on similar French institutions had also been established, bringing royal authority closer to the local level. At the same time, the powers of traditional corporate groups, whether of towns or nobility, were gradually assumed in greater quantity by direct royal officials, and the number of special semi-autonomous jurisdictions decreased. The influence of the nobility in government was also tempered somewhat by a gradual increase in the number of middle-class ministers and officials at the central level.

With the accession of Charles III in 1759, a new vigor was introduced into governmental reform. Aided by a succession of able and enlightened ministers—Floridablanca, d'Aranda, Campomanes, and Olavide—Charles not only reformed and tightened up the administration of the provincial intendancies, but also established for the first time, in 1783, a Council of State (*Junta del Estado*) that advised him on all matters of state and acted as a coordinating body between the Crown and the various administrative agencies. These agencies, too, were reformed, with a sharp de-emphasis on the numerous councils that had served earlier as heads of administrative departments, and which had functioned with a chaotic lack of communication with one another and with the Crown. The number of state secretaries serving as department heads was increased, and the older councils were deprived of more and more of their functions and powers.

In 1766, Charles also reformed municipal governments, giving all taxpayers a share of sorts in the election of communal deputies and the city syndic, or mayor, but at the same time tightening the relationship between the central government and the municipalities through more deliberate supervision of city affairs. By the time of Charles' death in 1788, the apparatus of royal government itself was more efficient than at any time in Spain's history, though still far from a model of rationality; and the king's government had virtually overcome all resistance by the traditional corporate representative assemblies, or *Cortés*.

Sweden

Since the early eighteenth century, when the disastrous foreign policy of Charles XII, the "Lion of the North," had led to the imposition of a severely restrictive constitution on the monarch, the conduct of Swedish government had lain largely in the hands of a Council of the Realm—dominated by the nobility —and the Swedish Diet, which represented nearly all classes of the population according to the division of four estates: nobility, clergy, burghers, and peasants. Faction, which was not always bound to a clash of different estates, quickly developed within both the Council and the Diet, and much of the internal history of Sweden from 1740 until 1772 concerns bitter domestic disputes over various social, economic, and political issues.

When Gustavus III ascended the throne in 1771, he was determined to revitalize royal authority and to make the monarch once again the effective ruler of the state. In 1772, in a sudden *coup d'état,* Gustavus abolished the Constitution of 1720 and imposed a new one formulated by himself. The Diet was adjourned with the promise that it would be recalled in six years —a promise that was honored in 1778. The king would retain a council; but it would advise, not govern. The Diet kept a number of important rights, especially in matters pertaining to war and finances. The king in fact had no intention of excluding the various estates entirely from the government; his desire was simply to make the king once again master in his own household, the real policy-maker.

His move came at an opportune time, and was not unwelcome to the estates, all of which tended to regard it as directed against their opponents. The nobility especially had come under increasingly heavy attack by commoners in the Diet before 1772, and they regarded the king as their saviour. Gustavus looked on the aristocracy as an ornament to his court and throne; but, for his advisors, he preferred newly ennobled and usually quite capable men rather than members of the older high aristocracy. He quickly improved the bureaucratic machinery of Sweden, removing and in some cases punishing negligent officials, improving the schedule of work, and modernizing various administrative offices. Finland, at this time part of the Swedish state, also received greater attention and was more closely integrated into the monarchy.

By the late 1780's, the nobility had become restive in its relative political inactivity and provided enough evidence of potentially revolutionary sentiments that Gustavus felt it necessary to increase and confirm his power by a second *coup,* represented in the Act of Union and Security of 1789. This was in effect a new constitution, in which virtually the only power partially withheld from the king was that of taxation. He summoned the estates to approve the Act after purchasing the support of the three lower orders by making concessions to the clergy on appointments and promotions, opening government positions to merit, abolishing restrictions on the purchase of hitherto privileged property, and liberalizing laws pertaining to the property and economic freedom of the peasantry (which was already personally free). The nobility, reprimanded and coerced into agreement to the new order, remained dissatisfied. It was their plotting that resulted in the assassination of Gustavus at a masquerade ball in 1792. In spite of his early death, however, Gustavus had raised the Crown to a commanding position that was passed along almost intact to his successors.

France

It is almost a truism that the French government for most of the eighteenth century before 1789 was distinguished less by reform than by the remarkable lack of it. The French monarchy in the halcyon days of Louis XIV (1643–1715) had one of the most complex, articulated, and efficient governmental systems in Europe—so impressive was it, in fact, that it served many other countries as a model. But after some unimpressive experiments at the central level by the Duke of Orleans, regent for Louis XV, the administrative structure of the kingdom remained almost unchanged until the Revolution. A number of central councils, all headed theoretically by the king, advised the monarch on various aspects of foreign and domestic affairs, while a small group of secretaries of state headed the administrative departments charged with implementing policy. At the provincial and local levels, royal officials known as intendants, outfitted with an extraordinarily wide range of supervisory and police functions, including some judicial powers, carried on most government business, aided by subordinate staffs of varying size.

Throughout the eighteenth century, such changes as occurred in French administration were the result mainly of a slow evolution of independence on the part of many intendants, a development that was encouraged by a certain lethargy among many of the supervisory organs at the center, as well as by the generally only fitful interest in day-to-day government business shown by the self-indulgent Louis XV. Among the intendants were many men of unusual capability and enlightenment, who gradually assumed a more executive character and extended the scope of their duties to compensate for the failures of the central government. The greatest energy and reform-mindedness for much of this period was not to be found as much in formal alterations of governmental structures as in the slow elaboration of reforms on the local and provincial levels, with the frequent establishment of a community of interest and cooperation between the intendants and traditional authorities—such as the municipalities and, in some cases, the provincial nobility.

Two specific reforms after 1770 that affected the structure of government were of some temporary importance, however. The first was the exile and dismissal of the great *parlement* of Paris, a measure executed by Chancellor Maupeou with the approval of Louis XV. The *parlement*, a judicial body composed of nobles whose ancestors had bought their positions on the court, with the right to transmit them to their posterity, regarded itself as the conscience of the kingdom: It could not legislate or veto royal decrees; but by tradition, it had the right to register decrees before their execution and to remonstrate with the king when they felt decrees to be in violation of the traditional constitution or the best interests of the country. Though they put themselves forward as the defenders of the people, the *parlementaires* in fact constituted a closed and self-interested corporation, obstinately opposed to any reform that might lessen the privileges enjoyed by their class.

By the late 1760's, the *parlement* of Paris had become particularly obnoxious, refusing to register decrees, ordering the arrest and trial of royal officials, and spreading seditious protests through the land by means of pamphlets. Worse yet, it was being imitated by the dozen provincial *parlements* scattered around the kingdom. In 1771, Maupeou dissolved the *parlements* by royal order and proceeded to set up a series of "superior councils" to perform the judicial business hitherto assigned to the *parlements*. This very important reform could have cleared the way for a major series of social and financial reforms, had it only remained. But when Louis XVI came to the throne in 1774, the *parlements* were reinstated by the young king in a vain attempt to court the popularity and support that his predecessor had so notably forfeited. Benevolent and pious, but also naive and mentally undistinguished, Louis thereby re-created one of the greatest obstructions to the progress of badly needed reform in his kingdom.

The immense unpopularity and mistrust that characterized popular attitudes towards the government was in fact a major obstacle to reform, no matter how beneficial it might be. In an attempt to salvage the reputation of the government and to bring home the necessity of reform to the socially important groups of the kingdom, the Director-General of Finance between 1776 and 1781, the Swiss banker Jacques Necker, utilizing an idea originally recommended by Turgot (Controller-General of Finance, 1774–76), proposed the establishment of provincial advisory assemblies; these would be composed of notable men of all classes in the area and would cooperate with the government in its administration of public works of all kinds. Two such assemblies were actually set up, in 1778 and 1779, and immediately began their work of assisting the government. Thereafter, the plan stalled and was not raised again until an extension of the assemblies to the whole country was proposed as part of a sweeping reform program by another Controller-General, Calonne, in 1786-87. Calonne's reforms, the last major ones proposed before the Revolution, were all rejected by a combination of opposition from the *parlements* and a special Assembly of Notables, consisting mostly of nobles, in 1787. This potentially beneficial administrative reform therefore also fell victim to the interests of the privileged orders of the kingdom, and the government structure remained unchanged until the Revolution.

Other Countries

Two smaller states—Portugal and Denmark-Norway—deserve mention because of the activity of important ministers who, while not technically the heads of state, so dominated their monarchs that they became virtual dictators while they were in office. In Portugal, the death of the imbecilic John V in 1750 caused the Queen-Regent to call the capable and courageous Marquis de Pombal as Secretary of State. Pombal acquired such an ascendancy over the young King Joseph I that he was able to control the country until the King's death in 1777. Some of Pombal's reforms will be discussed under other headings below. As concerns government and administration, however, Pombal virtually liberated the state from the excessive influence of church and nobility and made possible a truly independent royal policy—under his aegis, of course. He carried through an extensive policy of administrative reform in 1761, involving the suppression of some offices that were both useless and expensive and the improvement and better coordination of others. His fall from power in 1777 did not prevent a continuation of the benefits derived from the successes of his administrative work.

Johann Frederick Struensee in the Kingdom of Denmark-Norway attained a position similar to that of Pombal in Portugal. As personal physician to the mentally incompetent Christian VII (1766–1808) and the lover of his Queen, Struensee managed to insinuate himself into the government and with the permission of the mad King, abolished the important Privy Council that had allowed the nobility to exercise a predominant control on the conduct of government. By then assuming the right to issue cabinet orders in the King's name but without the royal signature, he made himself head of the cabinet and a virtual dictator. A Prussian by birth, he reorganized the Danish administration along a Prussian pattern, with close centralization of political and judicial authorities, abolition of older administrative organs and creation of new ones, and introduction of precision and clarity in state business. He also increased the rapidity of state business, reduced royal favoritism, and established an examination system to serve as a standard for appointment to public office in place of the previous system of appointment by birth or favor.

Struensee's opposition gathered forces quickly and persuaded the witless King to order his arrest after only eighteen months in office. The furious pace of Struensee's reforms—he issued more than 600 edicts during his brief tenure—had confused and alienated the sympathies of many who had originally supported him; after a parody of a trial, in which the hapless young man implicated the Queen in his crimes (or better, vices), he was executed in 1772. A period of reaction followed until, in 1784, the able and enlightened A. P. Bernstorff was called to office and picked up some of the threads of Struensee's reforms, which he then continued in a slower and more realistic fashion.

Many other lesser states, too numerous and in many cases too tiny to mention, could also be cited as examples of the attention paid by monarchs and ministers in this period to the reform of the institutions of government. Bernardo Tanucci, chief minister of the Kingdom of the Two Sicilies from 1759–76, was a reformer of some note, as were Charles August, Duke of Saxony-Weimar from 1775 to 1828; Charles Frederick, Margrave of Baden from 1746 to 1811; and a number of small princelings, ecclesiastical and secular, elsewhere in Europe.

ECONOMIC AND FISCAL REFORM

The development of economic life in Europe in the later eighteenth century remained under that close supervision and control by the state that had been the earmark of political economy since the seventeenth century. In all countries, mercantile protectionism continued to shape economic policy, with the result that tariff barriers to foreign manufactures, stringent controls on commerce, and state and private monopolies, subsidies, and tax remissions all encouraged export industries and protected domestic manufacturers of products that rulers did not wish their states to have to import.

The degree of governmental paternalism in all sectors of the economy varied from one country to another, but was characteristically strong in nearly all. In some instances, the amount and pace of state intervention increased markedly after 1760 or so; in others, it remained fairly steady or even declined somewhat. Frederick II of Prussia and Pombal in Portugal are both noteworthy for the furious pace of their direct subventions for numerous domestic industries, as well as for their increased monopolizations—salt, coffee, and tobacco as state enterprises in Frederick's case and commercial companies and the Portuguese wine industry in Pombal's. Strengthened prohibitive and protective economic policies with regard to imports, in addition to this encouragement of export industries, were especially important in Austria under Joseph II as well. All countries remained formally committed to numerous mercantilistic expedients throughout this period.

While much government intervention took the form of restriction, some not unimportant steps were taken to increase the freedom of commerce and manufactures. One of the most important of these was an assault on the restrictive influence of the guilds, whose traditional privileges were increasingly recognized as detrimental to the development and expansion of new methods of production, controlled by a rising class of non-guild manufacturers. Since, in general and with some significant exceptions, the fiscal interest of the state was primarily concerned with the quantity of production rather than the quality of goods produced or the welfare of the guild members, rulers took various measures to attempt the reduction of the economic influence of the guilds. In numerous German states, in Tuscany, in Spain, Austria, and Sweden, princes undertook to revise guild statutes, subordinate guild organizations to government supervision, expand their exclusive membership, decrease their monopoly privileges, or to abolish them entirely. In France, Turgot and his successors fought for their abolition, but with little success. In other countries, however, increased freedom for manufactures did result, and in turn helped to nudge production figures upwards.

Freedom of internal commerce was another reform eagerly solicited by many manufacturers and merchants, and one that made some headway under the administrations of the "enlightened" monarchs. Restrictions and tolls on the movement of goods within one and the same country came to be seen as major hindrances to consumption, and therefore also to production. Joseph II created something of a free-trade area in his Austrian and Bohemian lands to facilitate the exchange of goods, while his brother Leopold between 1766 and 1782 created a unified toll and customs area out of virtually all of his Grand Duchy of Tuscany. Catherine II of Russia and a series of controllers-general in France had some success with similar policies, while Charles III of Spain not only freed most internal trade, but in 1778 also greatly relaxed commercial restrictions between Spanish ports and the Spanish New World colonies. One particularly interesting facet of this new freedom in trade was that accorded to grain and agricultural produce, which will be discussed below.

Few attempts of any real importance were made to implement free trade between nations. Gustavus III tried an interesting scheme to test the effects of freedom on economic life by designating the small town of Marstrand, on an island near Göteborg, as a completely free emporium where domestic and foreign goods could be imported free and exported at only a small fee. He later established other free cities and markets in out-of-the-way places in Finland and the outer Swedish provinces, but all of these were little more than amusements to the experimental mind of the Swedish king and had no observable effect on the Swedish economy. In 1786, France and England concluded a commercial treaty that drastically reduced import tariffs of the two countries on an enumerated series of items; but its effect, for France at least, was not such as to encourage any more excursions into the realm of free trade, since French demand for cheap English manufactured goods far outweighed English demand for French silks and wines and resulted in an immediate and ruinous decline of many infant French manufactures.

The primary importance of agriculture in the economy of all European countries in this period was naturally reflected in the extraordinary vigor with which monarchs attempted to reform this sector of economic life. The variety of particular measures designed to increase production from the land defies enumeration, and of course these differed according to the circumstances of each country. Expansion of the amount of land under cultivation was perhaps most successfully pursued in Prussia, Spain, and Russia. Frederick II drained extensive areas of swamp, especially around the lower Oder and Vistula Rivers, and attracted many colonists from Germany and other countries— nearly 300,000 by the end of his reign—to occupy and cultivate the reclaimed land.

Charles III, faced with an overwhelming stagnancy in Spanish agriculture, sought to limit the extension of *mayorazgos*, or entailed estates, which by law could not be sold by their owners, but which also could not be developed because of a lack of capital. He broke up some of these and distributed their un-developed land to peasants; his successors were able to forbid the foundation of any new *mayorazgos* in 1789. Charles also freed some of the vast tracts of pasture held by the *mesta*, the sheep-raising combine, for purposes of grain cultivation; again, the *mesta* was entirely suppressed shortly after his death in 1792. One of Charles' most famous experiments was his founda-tion of agricultural colonies in the barren Sierra Morena hills, for which he attracted colonists from foreign countries. Intended to operate according to the laws of Nature and under the direct in-fluence of Physiocratic doctrine, these colonies proved to be fail-ures. Somewhat more successful were the efforts of Catherine II, who gave very generous conditions to foreigners to settle huge tracts of thinly populated lands in Russia.

To these efforts at reclamation and colonization of lands was added a movement towards the partition of village common lands among individual peasants, under the assumption that such lands would be used for the cultivation of cash crops, rather than as the common pasture and woodland that they had been pre-viously. The great interest shown by monarchs and princes all over Europe in the introduction of new agricultural techniques and soil-restoring measures had to do not merely with improve-ment of the soil as such, but also with the reduction of the amount of land that had to be left fallow at any given planting in order to allow it to regain its fertility. The amount of land thus reclaimed from fallow probably exceeded, in the long run, the total reclaimed from swamp and forest.

In order to spread knowledge of agricultural improvements throughout the agrarian population, governments encouraged the foundation of private agricultural societies in various provincial and local areas and, in some cases, created societies of their own. France had not only an Agricultural Society of some im-portance for a time, but also established a separate Ministry of Agriculture; while in Spain, direct royal encouragement of societies of "Friends of the Country" and other economic associa-tions attracted a considerable membership, which in some cases sponsored chairs of agriculture and economics in the universities and technical schools. Royal academies and philosophical societies in many countries were urged to develop an interest in practical agricultural matters; and they offered premiums and prizes for new inventions, essays on agricultural management, and so on. The establishment of model farms in many places also provided an opportunity for the testing of new techniques and the instruction of visitors; many such model estates were set up by private individuals, but Charles III, Frederick II, and Catherine II were only a few of the monarchs who devoted some part of their crown lands to such experiments.

The failure of the vast majority of cultivators everywhere to adopt very many of these improvements was not just a result of a lack of communication. Peasants, of course, remained largely uninformed in spite of occasionally herculean efforts of local officials, or even village priests and landlords, to enlighten them. But even the informed among the upper landowning classes simply did not have the capital to undertake improvements on any large scale; and a lack of credit possibilities in all but a few favored areas of Europe, mostly in the west and northwest, made it impossible to borrow except at ruinous interest rates. Some monarchs, recognizing the tremendous importance of credit and its virtual unavailability in the private sector, began to sponsor different kinds of credit facilities. The foundation of royal banks and other public or semi-public credit institutions can be seen in Spain, Russia, Prussia, and Austria, while already existing facilities in more advanced countries underwent expansion and refinement.

Among other expedients designed to increase agricultural production was the tendency to free the cultivator from restrictions on his labor, utilization of the land, and the sale of his produce. Since improvement of the peasant's legal and economic status will be dealt with in another context later, let it suffice here to point to very extensive experiments in numerous states with freedom of the grain trade. In a sense, greater freedom in the movement of foodstuffs was only one part of a general reduction of restrictions on commerce in this period. But many more states tried freedom of the grain trade than freedom in the movement of manufactured commodities. Not a single major state, and very few minor ones, failed to decree one or another degree of free movement of grain internally, primarily to the end of assuring as steady a price level as possible for foodstuffs, thus eliminating both famine and vast surplusses and hopefully making possible agricultural profits that could be used to improve and expand cultivation. On the whole, these efforts reacted beneficially on agriculture, though traditional fears of famine and other factors combined to make such policies always tentative and subject to immediate recall. In France, for example, free trade was decreed in 1754, in 1763, in 1774, and in some later years—always to be revoked shortly thereafter; in other states, freedom was often granted to the grain trade only for a specified number of years. In all cases and at all times, the possibility of a reassertion of state control lurked in the background.

As the economy prospered, so did the state treasury. The means of their interconnection was, of course, taxation; and no concern of any monarch in this period was stronger than that pertaining to the fiscal system, whose revenues underlay all state policy. The fiscal preoccupation of rulers was not new to the eighteenth century; but after 1760 or so, the review and reform—or attempts at reform—of taxes and tax structures present a dynamic picture that is at some contrast to a generally more static condition of tax systems in the first half of the century. The greater interest of states in their fiscal situations was signalized by numerous general economic surveys undertaken after the end of the Seven Years' War in 1763 and by a widespread establishment or revision of tax assessment lists, especially the cadasters (land rolls), which were used to determine exemptions, land values, and so on.

An almost universal reform of fiscal administrative agencies occurred as part of the governmental reforms discussed above. One of the first institutions to come under scrutiny was the so-called "tax farm," an arrangement of renting the collection of (indirect) taxes to private individuals or groups, who advanced the government the total sum anticipated from the taxes concerned and who were then allowed to keep all or part of whatever they could squeeze out of the people in excess of the government's estimated revenues. The single advantage of this arrangement, apart from saving the government the administrative task of collection, was that it enabled governments to reckon part of the next year's budget with a definite sum—the advance given by the tax farmers. Its disadvantages lay in the dissatisfaction the farmers awakened among the people by their often heavyhanded methods, as well as in the losses of revenue the government might suffer by failing to do its own collection. Whether reform now meant the establishment of new and more efficient tax farms or the abolition of some or all farming arrangements depended on the circumstances of particular states.

Frederick II created a special Excise and Tolls Department (sometimes called the French *Régie*) in 1766 and charged it with the administration and collection of most indirect taxes. With a staff of 2,000 officials, of whom about 200 were French, this department made itself unpopular for the next twenty years by its efficiency, which was guaranteed by Frederick's contract to pay a percentage of the taxes collected to the administrative head of the *Régie*, a French tax farmer named de Launay. While the Prussian scheme was not really a renting of the taxes, other countries, especially some of the Italian states, developed fullblown tax farms in imitation of the best-known example, that of France.

In Tuscany, on the other hand, Leopold revoked the general farm of taxes in 1768 because of its wastefulness and corruption, set up new administrative bodies, and was thereby able not only to increase revenues but also to reduce taxes and to gain more accurate knowledge of the economic and financial condition of the country. Charles III also curtailed the activities of tax farmers in Naples and Sicily. Even in France, where the worst features of the system had long since come to predominate, but where it appeared to be ineradicable, controllers-general advocated curtailment or abolition of the general farm; and, under Necker, its scope actually was limited somewhat. In other countries, the establishment of permanent salaried officials and a streamlining of bureaucratic organizations contributed to lessen corruption and overlapping functions. Many administrative innovations, such as the creation of officials in Austria and Spain to supervise municipal finances more closely and in other cases to restrict the tax-granting privileges of traditional representative corporations, were also directly related to the fiscal interests of the state.

The eternal search for new sources of revenue also led monarchs to reevaluate the fiscal position of the privileged orders of society. The policies of Catholic rulers with regard to church property were greatly influenced by fiscal considerations. The restriction of church ownership of property was in large measure prompted by the desire to prohibit the extension of mortmain, not merely because it was unfavorable to the development of the economy as a whole, but also because church land was traditionally exempt from taxation. Even more drastic steps, such as the final secularization of all church land in Russia by Catherine II or the dissolution of monasteries by Joseph II in Austria, brought substantially increased revenues to the state. Piecemeal reduction of numerous specific ecclesiastical exemptions was accomplished almost everywhere in Catholic Europe as another method of tapping the enormous wealth of the clergy. There were also a few attempts—almost uniformly unsuccessful—to impose a small direct tax on ecclesiastical incomes.

Nor did the landowning gentry or nobility escape the sharp eye of rulers and their fiscal advisors. Because of great variations in the taxability of the gentry in different countries, it is difficult to speak of truly uniform trends in the fiscal policies of monarchs in this period in their attempts to modify the traditional exemptions of the nobility, except to say that an increase in its financial contribution to the state was everywhere solicited. The frequent prohibition of incorporation of peasant tenures into lords' domains in Prussia, Austria, and elsewhere was partly intended to preserve the taxability of these peasant lands, while Charles III's breakup of entailed estates had the effect of creating new peasant tenures subject to a higher rate of taxation. Single and direct land taxes—some of them stimulated by the Physiocratic idea of the *impôt unique,* a tax that would be equally applicable to all proprietors—were attempted or seriously considered in Spain, Sweden, Austria, and France at one time or another; but all failed eventually, due to the opposition of privileged interests and administrative difficulties. Small income taxes, similarly, were imposed in a number of countries; they had somewhat greater success, perhaps; but increases were stubbornly opposed by the privileged orders, which also made impossible any realization of more modern schemes such as the progressive income tax mentioned (but not tried) by Frederick II in his *Political Testament* of 1768.

The results of the economic and fiscal policies and expedients described above were as varied as the situations of the countries where they were executed. Probably the most notable failures occurred in France, where after 1774 no major reforms were allowed to continue for more than a few months. From Turgot to Necker to Calonne, Brienne, and back to Necker again, the number of beneficial changes proposed was enormous; but the financial disarray of the country and the furious opposition of the higher groups in society to any measures that smacked of higher taxes or reduced privileges made an impossible task out of an already difficult one. Reform here did not fail; it simply did not occur. On the other hand, the private sector of the French economy was a relatively advanced and, on balance, a healthy one in the years preceding the Revolution, so that while the fiscal crisis of the government indeed impeded progress, it did not halt it.

In almost every other country, the results of government policies were good, if not always spectacular. The government of Portugal went heavily into debt as a result of Pombal's policies, and without getting the great economic growth he sought; but even here, the private sector of the economy showed gains that in the long run probably at least offset state losses. Spanish improvements, too, did not justify the great hopes of Charles III and his advisors, though it is easy to overlook the very real progress in industry, transportation, currency reform, and some aspects of agriculture, which clearly left Spain in better shape at the time of Charles' death than it had been at his accession.

In Prussia, Frederick II's prohibitive policies may have impeded progress in some areas of the economy, especially in the last years of his reign; but the energetic entrepreneurs who complained about these policies in the 1780's owed their own development to them. The state treasury during Frederick's reign more than doubled its revenues and, at the time of his death, had a surplus nearly three times its annual income. The economic policies of Maria Theresa and Joseph II in Austria led to an increase in industrial production that, as in Prussia, was small by comparison with figures from France or England, but was quite considerable by comparison with earlier conditions in the same country. Joseph's fiscal policies resulted in a tremendous reduction of the state debt and even a balanced budget in one year, 1786. New international involvements almost immediately wiped out any prospect of surplusses, however, and the failure or revocation of a number of tax measures after his death once again introduced a precarious element into state finances. The more solid contributions to the development of industry remained intact.

Joseph's brother Leopold was almost as much concerned about balanced budgets as was Joseph, and he succeeded in redeeming nearly three-quarters of the Tuscan state debt during his reign. Behind this was Leopold's conviction that private funds invested in the state could be employed more beneficially in productive enterprises than in state debentures. By increasing investment in industry and agriculture and in effect terminating the absolute dominance of Florence in the Tuscan economy, Leopold raised the economic condition of his entire realm. In contrast to the almost fanatical preoccupation with the reduction of ruinously large state debts in many countries, Catherine II performed one of her greatest services for the Russian economy in creating a state debt by heavy borrowing from both domestic and foreign sources. In capital-poor Russia, such indebtedness was an indispensable requirement for greater government involvement in economic planning and development, which was in turn necessary for the growth of Russian industry. Her monetary policy, too, created for the first time a really stable currency system, whose importance quickly became apparent in commercial exchange.

The Czaritsa's policies in many ways hindered the development of free enterprise, primarily through her patronage and encouragement of noblemen who employed serf labor in industry; this made very precarious the position of middle-class entrepreneurs who were attempting to organize manufacturing with free wage labor. But here, as in Prussia and Austria, the ruler had to work towards improvement from an extremely backward starting point, utilizing whatever resources were at hand; and, no matter how much freedom might be given to the middle class, it was simply too small to be favored against the interests of the gentry, whose importance in the Russian state was more than merely economic. In the short run, at least, both mercantile and industrial sectors of the Russian economy benefitted noticeably from Catherine's methods.

The Scandinavian countries—Denmark-Norway and Sweden —had proportionately large and prosperous commercial middle classes throughout the eighteenth century. A more business-like administration of public finances in Denmark under Struensee —and later, Bernstorff—and in Sweden under Gustavus III, together with somewhat more liberalized commercial policies, made slight contributions to an already high level of prosperity. But more important than these in Denmark was the rapid reform of agrarian life in the late 1780's and 1790's, which, by freeing peasants from their lords' jurisdiction and enabling them to buy their land and establish separate holdings, created a much improved level of agricultural production. In Sweden, it speaks for the already highly developed nature of the commercial economy that a basic currency reform undertaken by Gustavus was probably the most important single economic measure, and one which removed the greatest grievance of private economic life.

RELIGIOUS REFORM

One of the great earmarks of the later eighteenth century in Europe was an impressive and self-conscious political movement towards the toleration of religious minorities. When Frederick II declared that in his dominions "all religions must be tolerated," he was merely giving early expression to a conviction that became standard for many rulers in his time. More a deist than anything else, Frederick permitted freedom of worship for all religions, made no attempt to extirpate Catholicism in Silesia, and in fact even built a Catholic church in Berlin named after St. Hedwig, the patron saint of Silesia. Quite similar were the attitudes of Catherine II of Russia, who also was not noted for her piety. In Lutheran Sweden, it was not until the 1740's that a limited religious freedom was granted even to Calvinists, who wished to settle and exercise a trade in Sweden. But in 1778, with Gustavus III's blessing, agitation began for a new religious toleration, which culminated in a royal decree of 1781 granting toleration to foreign Christians who had settled in Sweden and to their posterity. They were not to proselytize, however, or to have processions or establish religious houses (e.g., monasteries). Full civil rights except for those of office-holding or standing for election to the Diet were granted. According to another edict of 1782, Jews were to be allowed to settle and to exercise their religion freely in three specified Swedish towns.

In Catholic countries, formal toleration for non-Catholics was not the rule even in this period. One can, however, speak of the growth of a body of tolerant opinion and of a rather permissive attitude towards Protestants in countries such as Portugal, Spain, some of the lesser Italian and German states, and France; in the latter, Louis XVI finally gave a measure of legal toleration to Protestants in 1787 and, in the following year, appointed a commission to study the question of the Jews in France. The only major Catholic country where formal toleration was granted was Austria. As early as 1774, Joseph II had insisted that the expulsion of Protestants from the Alpine lands of the monarchy cease, and he was responsible for the granting of the first academic degrees to Protestants by the University of Vienna in 1778. Very soon after Maria Theresa's death, Joseph issued his famous Patent of Toleration (1781), which sanctioned private religious services for recognized denominations and opened the civil service, academic education, and teaching positions to Protestants. These measures were not adequate to guarantee full legal equality, much less social equality, to Protestants. But they represented a major step towards those goals, and were largely kept in force by Leopold II after 1790.

Since the Reformation, most Protestant rulers of Europe had succeeded in subordinating the churches in their territories to state control and supervision, with the result that the eighteenth century witnessed only minor changes in the relationship of these churches to the state. Frederick II's acquisition of Catholic Silesia prompted him in 1742 to set up a general ecclesiastical ordinance regulating very strictly the separation of temporal and spiritual powers; and Frederick, like Protestant rulers in Denmark, Sweden, and elsewhere, occasionally stepped into church affairs to quell disputes and arrange matters to his liking. Generally, however, the great reforms of the religious establishment in this period occurred in Catholic countries, where the position of the Church in relation to the state was much stronger and more independent.

One of the most commonly pursued goals of Catholic rulers was that of loosening the tie of their territorial churches to Rome. Charles III in Spain in 1766 specified that the Inquisition might not execute any order from Rome without his prior authorization through the Council of Castile; Joseph II forbade appeals to Rome from Austrian state and church jurisdictions in matters of marriage; and Leopold, as early as 1768–69, directed that orders from Rome to any ecclesiastical authority in Tuscany go first to the government for approval. Later, Leopold tried to organize a series of territorial church councils that would in fact, if not in theory, have resulted in a large measure of independence for the Tuscan church from Rome. Some rulers required accounts of church moneys sent to Rome to be submitted to the government. Others, like Pombal in Portugal, expelled papal nuncios and in many other ways limited severely the kinds of appeals that could be made to Rome from ecclesiastical tribunals, religious foundations, and so on. In this as in other aspects of church-state relations, the amount of reform undertaken in any particular country often depended very much on how successful earlier rulers had been in adjusting relationships in their favor.

Of even greater concern than the connection with Rome was the question of the regulation of ecclesiastical administration, finances, and property. In almost all Catholic states, rulers attempted successfully to assert greater control over ecclesiastical appointments, to restrict the competence of church tribunals, and to eliminate various privileges that had exempted church personnel from state jurisdiction. The Inquisition was abolished in Tuscany and sharply curtailed in Portugal, Spain, and several Italian states, while ecclesiastical control of the education of church personnel came under closer government supervision; in some cases—Austria, for example—clerical training was actually placed under state control. The quality of the episcopate and of the discipline of monasteries and nunneries was also subjected to the supervision of the secular authorities.

Interference in church ritual, ceremony, and even creed was not uncommon. Pombal made a Jansenist catechism obligatory in Portugal—a measure censured and forbidden by Rome—while Grand Duke Leopold more or less openly encouraged the Jansenist faction in the Tuscan church. Joseph II forbade religious processions, dictated a simpler ritual, struck numerous religious holidays from the calendar, and discouraged religious displays of all kinds. Superstition, which was in some instances openly tolerated, not to say encouraged, by local clergy, was to be combatted, and rulers and their ministers commanded that religious and moral instruction be of a high level and not such as to cater to the credulousness of the common folk.

In a number of countries, the educational functions of the clergy were removed or reduced. The consequent assumption of such duties by lay authorities was made both possible and necessary by the expulsion of the Jesuits, who in many places had had primary responsibility and supervision of education at all levels. A wealthy order—and an extremely influential one—with traditionally close ties to Rome, the Society of Jesus was widely disliked by jealous and suspicious non-Jesuit churchmen and by statesmen for a number of reasons. Pombal forced the expulsion of the order from Portugal in 1759, ostensibly because of their supposed connection with an attempt on the king's life, but actually because of their opposition to his domestic and colonial policies. France expelled them in 1764, partly on the excuse of their failure to cover debts of a bankrupt Jesuit mission in Martinique, but actually because of the suspicions of the French court and the hatred of the Paris *parlement*, packed with Jansenists who loathed the Jesuits. Charles III of Spain followed suit in 1767, after being convinced by the anti-Jesuit faction at court that the Jesuits were fomenting riots and planning to murder him.

By 1769, Parma and the Kingdom of the Two Sicilies had also ousted the order. The final blow to the unfortunate Jesuits came with the election of Clement XIV to the papal throne, also in 1769; subjected to various threats and pressures from France and Spain, and indebted to some extent to the Austrian court for his election, Clement dissolved the order entirely in 1773. It was not to be revived again until the next century. In many cases, the funds and property confiscated from the Jesuits were administered for public purposes by the state.

The monastic orders fared little better than the Jesuits. They were frequently disliked by the secular clergy for their independence from episcopal control and were regarded as economically parasitic by the state. In Russia, Catherine II forbade the foundation of new monastic houses, while in other states the approval of the government was made obligatory for new houses. More rigid discipline in monasteries was ordered in Spain and Tuscany, to the end of reducing the number of monks and applicants, who, it was thought, might find the religious life less appealing if they were actually forced to live it. In some places, governments asserted their right to control the number of novitiates.

The mendicant (begging) orders often appeared to rulers to represent an especially indefensible phenomenon on economic, religious, and disciplinary grounds, and were severely restricted. The dissolution of monasteries in the lands of the Austrian crown was begun on a large scale by Joseph II, who suppressed nearly 800 houses during his reign; those engaged in useful charitable work—nursing and education, for example—were allowed to remain, but the property of others was confiscated and held in a special Religious Fund, created in 1782 to meet the financial demands of the pastoral obligations of the secular clergy. A notable feature of Joseph's religious policy was his care to see that the number of parishes be increased to provide for a closer contact of the secular priesthood with the common people; for Joseph believed that the secular clergy, if properly trained, could be an agent of much moral and political good to the ignorant peasant.

Finally, the regulation of church property in more direct

ways formed a consistent trend of state policy in this period. Taxation of lands owned by the Church, previously exempt, was introduced in some places, while in others, where exemption remained, there were attempts to limit the amount of property the Church could own or acquire. In Portugal, Pombal placed a limitation on religious bequests, and in Spain, France, and Austria, acquisition of land by the Church, whether by purchase or bequest, was made legally subject to the approval of secular authority. Catherine II, continuing policies begun under Peter I, secularized all church land and transformed the clergy into servants of the state. Again, in Protestant countries, the immense church-state problem relating to property did not exist, since the secularization and control of church property by the state had generally been the rule since the Reformation.

LEGAL AND JUDICIAL REFORM

The reform of law and its administration in the various states of Europe must be looked at fully within the context of more general attempts to rationalize and unify the framework of public life. The monarchies that existed in the eighteenth century were political units whose character was determined by a process of patchwork accrual of bits and pieces of territory extending generations or centuries into the past. Each of these territories possessed traditional laws and institutions that were often left partly or wholly intact when they were incorporated into larger states. As a result, the legal systems of any one country could and did show a great variety of codes, procedures, and administrative and judicial institutions whose coexistence was a fertile source of confusion and expense.

One remedy widely attempted in the eighteenth century was that of unification and codification of the body of laws obtaining in any single ruler's dominions. In Austria, a codification of criminal law was completed in 1768 under the supervision of Maria Theresa and Joseph II, and was revised and supplemented by a new penal code under Joseph's sole direction in the 1780's. Codification of civil law was also begun, but was not completed until 1811. Prussian jurists under the leadership of such figures as von Cocceji, von Carmer, and Suarez began work in the 1740's on a unified law code for the Prussian monarchy, which was finally completed and put into practice in 1794. Only in a few other minor states, such as Bavaria and Tuscany, were results as successful as those of Austria and Prussia. Catherine II's famous convocation of a legislative assembly in 1767, which represented the nobility, the towns, and other groups in Russian society, was the most spectacular failure among numerous well-intentioned but ineffective attempts at fundamental revision of the entire system of laws. The Empress drew up a most enlightened *Instruction* to serve as a general guide for the delegates, who were to create an entirely new code of laws; their deliberations quickly bogged down in detail and argumentation, however, and finally ceased altogether. Spanish reformers also made some weak attempts to introduce a new code, but to little effect, while in Spanish-ruled Naples and Sicily, even the competent Bernardo Tanucci made little headway against the eleven inherited law codes that oppressed the country. A commission of jurists appointed late in Louis XVI's reign to study legal reform in France barely made its initial recommendations before the Revolution began.

The reform of legal procedures that accompanied these codifications all tended towards the simplification and shortening of the judicial process—whether by substituting oral for written procedure, eliminating the lengthy process of sending documents to university law faculties for opinions, or by various other means. Codification itself, of course, as in the case of the Prussian *Landrecht* of 1794, usually helped to shorten litigation by simplifying and clarifying statute law. The quality of judges was also improved in many places by higher standards of judicial appointment and by payment of higher salaries, thus reducing temptations to corruption from bribery or inflated fees.

Reform of judicial administration was of major importance in a few places. Joseph II undertook the most comprehensive reorganization, which introduced for the first time in Hapsburg lands something resembling a truly unified court system. The abolition of the French *parlements* in 1771, which we have mentioned earlier, was primarily a political measure, but was followed by a much improved system of royal courts. The recall of the *parlements* by Louis XVI in 1774 put an end to reformers' hopes until 1788, when, in one of his few moments of decisiveness, Louis again decreed the abolition of the *parlements,* the creation of a new supreme court for the registration of decrees, and the establishment of 47 grand districts for the settlement of civil and criminal litigation. Once again, however, the entire plan was revoked when the decision was made to call the Estates-General.

One particularly interesting feature of judicial reform was the more or less deliberate attempt to separate judicial from administrative functions or, which was not quite the same thing, to secure a measure of independence for the judiciary. In Central and eastern Europe, particularly, the performance of judicial functions was a normal adjunct of many administrative offices, and many bureaucrats were required to have some degree of legal training for their posts. An inevitable feature of this system was a tendency for officials to use their judicial powers as an instrument for the achievement of their administrative goals, without due regard to the dictates of impartial justice. In Prussia, Austria, Tuscany, Spain, and a few of the lesser German states, measures were taken to limit the judicial competence of administrative bodies and to expand regular courts to take over affairs previously handled by administrators.

The separation of the judiciary was probably best institutionalized in Austria under Maria Theresa, with Joseph in somewhat reluctant agreement; but it was Frederick II who most clearly enunciated the philosophy of separation, stating on several occasions that the ruler must not interfere in the course of legal proceedings: "in the courts of law the laws must speak and the ruler must remain silent." Frederick and other rulers made real efforts to reduce their own intervention in judicial affairs, and while always insisting on their sovereign supervisory functions and their right to review sentences, they nonetheless allowed a much greater measure of real judicial independence than had previously existed.

The period of "enlightened despotism" also witnessed some changes in the harshness of criminal codes, procedures, and punishments. The widely published work of the Italian Cesare Beccaria, *Of Crimes and Punishments* (1764), together with an increasing number of similar works by others, undoubtedly helped to produce this more enlightened approach to penology. Beccaria had argued, among other things, that torture as a method of extracting accurate information or true confessions was both inhuman and ineffective, since a prisoner under enough pain would be likely to say anything to put an end to his agony; that punishments ought to be better fitted to the crimes committed, and, specifically, that the death penalty, then applied to many very minor crimes, ought to be reserved only for major ones; and that the certainty of punishment was a more effective deterrent to crime than its severity.

Sharp restrictions on the use of torture occurred everywhere in Europe, beginning in the 1760's, and in many cases it was formally and completely abolished. Death penalties were meted out with greater reservation, and particularly cruel penalties, such as death by drowning for infanticide, were eliminated. In at least one instance, Tuscany, capital punishment was entirely done away with, though it was later reinstated because of some serious civil disturbances. The elimination of penalties such as the confiscation of a criminal's property or loss of title, which worked a hardship as much on the family as on the criminal himself, also helped to humanize penal codes, while the revision of law codes at the same time entirely suppressed various laws relating to witchcraft, sorcery, the begetting of children out of wedlock, and other "crimes" of similar nature.

Finally, a beginning was made in the reform of prisons, though a great deal more was written about it than done. The influence of the Englishman John Howard, whose disquieting *State of the Prisons* (1777) and *Account of the Principal Lazarettos* (1789) were widely circulated through Europe, can be seen in a number of governmental surveys of prisons of the late 1770's and 1780's. Louis XVI and his minister Malesherbes, who had jurisdiction of prisons, made several direct pleas to prison governors to ease the lot of their charges, and a number of intendants showed an interest in both construction and improvement of prisons. Unfortunately, the American war interfered with what was by 1778 beginning to become a real movement towards reform.

EDUCATIONAL REFORM

Among the particularly outstanding characteristics of the period of "enlightened despotism" was a marked increase in the interest shown in the expansion of educational facilities of one kind or another. The diffusion of useful knowledge could be accomplished in many ways. Real freedom of the press existed almost nowhere, but many monarchs deliberately relaxed censorship regulations to permit the publication or sale of books and pamphlets that contained useful information or ideas tending to support their own reforms. A formal abolition of censorship was decreed by Struensee in Denmark in 1770, however; and in Sweden, a law of freedom of the press was revised and liberalized by Gustavus III after his *coup d'état,* though a reappearance of party strife in the last years of his reign led to increased restrictions on that freedom.

Other rulers, such as Charles III and Joseph II, quite consciously supported the diffusion of enlightened publications—even when they did not agree with them—as a method of attacking the ideological position of privileged groups, especially the clergy, whose opposition to reforms placed serious hindrance in the path of their realization. In a few cases, monarchs played an active role in subsidizing publication: Charles III virtually created the enlightened periodical press in Spain, while Catherine II licensed a number of private publishing houses in Russia to translate and publish Western books. In Tuscany, Leopold gave considerable material assistance to a group of men interested in reprinting the famous French *Encyclopédie* in Italian; he even recommended that they imitate the original Paris edition rather than the abridged and somewhat sterilized Lucca edition, but they chose the latter anyway, knowing perhaps better than the Grand Duke himself just how novel and daring their subscribers and readers would permit them to be.

The number of royal academies and societies founded or expanded in this period is too large to enumerate. Some, of course, had already existed for a long time; but in all cases, a notable trend towards greater preoccupation with practical subjects—

science, mechanics, economics, and agriculture, for example—can be discerned, as well as a tendency towards their conversion into organs for the elaboration and propagation of enlightened ideas. Private societies, too, such as those devoted to agricultural improvement, flourished in every country and through their connection with administrative agencies, technical schools, and other public institutions made significant contributions to the increase and application of useful knowledge.

A great deal of interest in formal institutions of instruction at all levels not only led to the creation of special schools for the children of nobles in such places as Portugal and Russia, designed to promote the creation of a more highly trained official class, but eventuated also in some major reforms in universities and other institutions of higher learning. Both Spain and Austria provide excellent examples of increased state control of universities, especially after the expulsion of the Jesuits. In Austria, supervision of the University of Vienna, which was still run as a semi-independent medieval corporation, was taken over by the government, which not only assumed its financial responsibilities, but opened doors to rationalism by such measures as charging the teaching of canon law and church history to members of the law faculty rather than to ecclesiastics. The Spanish Crown asserted its control over universities through the establishment of commissioners to supervise the authority of university rectors in 1769, and through regulation of examinations and degrees and the right of appointment of professors in 1769–70. Pedagogical institutes and religious seminaries, both of which trained teachers, were similarly removed from exclusive church control, where that was the case, or, where they were already state institutions, were more closely supervised and subjected to higher standards. In these schools, both the quality of students and the character of the curriculum underwent revision to increase the capacity of teachers to give instruction in vocational subjects in addition to reading, writing, and religion.

Popular or mass education became a real concern of governments for almost the first time in this period. In all cases, the general movement was towards systems subsidized and supervised or wholly controlled by the state. School attendance for children of certain ages was made obligatory in Prussia, Austria, and a few other states, though enforcement of this requirement was often very difficult. Compulsory attendance was a bit premature in any case, since financial considerations and a lack of qualified teachers, together with a considerable amount of hostility and resistance among peasants and others, made all but rudimentary progress in the erection of comprehensive primary school systems an impossibility. Various plans for the distribution of schoolbooks to children without charge and for other measures to ease the burden of education for the lower classes achieved little success.

State control of education at this level, too, was extended to curriculum, in which moral and religious instruction, good citizenship, hygiene, and occupational concerns predominated, usually at the expense of literature and other subjects of less everyday importance. Government control officials supervised the activities of schools as closely as they could; Leopold II of Austria was the only monarch who seriously thought of involving teachers and professors themselves in the formulation of educational policy, through associations that would meet to discuss books, methods, and curricula, and which would also constitute the supervisory organs for education. The plan was actually introduced by decree in 1790, but was quickly abandoned by Leopold's less liberal son and successor. These efforts at popular education, tentative and quantitatively slight though their results may have been in this time, nevertheless established patterns of theory and organization that were to be of great significance in the nineteenth century; they may not be dismissed as total failures.

SOCIAL REFORM

There was one major type of reform in the later eighteenth century that actually tended to alter the character of a social class. This was peasant reform, in which nearly all rulers expressed an interest at one time or another. Since the condition of peasants with regard to legal status, proprietary rights, and economic position varied immensely from one part of Europe to another and even within the same state, it will be possible to draw only the broadest outline of reform in the status of peasants. Central and eastern Europe were the regions where the overall status of the peasantry was lowest; it worsened, in general, from west to east across all of Europe. One or another form of personal dependence, precarious rights of tenure, and widespread poverty were the lot of the average peasant.

Beginning in the 1760's, a number of rulers undertook to abolish the unfree status of serfdom among their peasants. Apart from a few lesser monarchs, such as Margrave Charles Frederick of Baden, the most notable efforts were those of Maria Theresa and Joseph II in Austria, and A.P. Bernstorff and others as successors of Struensee in Denmark-Norway. In both monarchies, the personal servitude of peasants and their families was greatly restricted or abolished entirely. Other monarchs talked much about it, but did little to establish full legal freedom and personality for the peasantry. Frederick II on his crown lands assured his peasants of hereditary tenure and reduced their labor and financial obligations to him as landlord. He recommended imitation of his example to noble landowners as well, but in this, as in the question of serfdom, did not attempt coercion in this direction.

Joseph II went much further in this respect and, in 1789, decreed that crown and private peasants should pay no more than 30 percent of their total income to their landlords, of which 59 percent was rent and 41 percent land tax. In other countries— Tuscany and Spain, for example—the services and dues owed to the monarch as landlord were adjusted, and a quite general movement arose towards abolishing labor services in favor of cash payments. The famous proposals of Turgot and his successors to abolish the *corvée* in France—a peasant obligation to perform labor service for the Crown, usually on the royal roads, for a certain number of days each year—were intended not only to make all proprietors, including landlords, share in the upkeep of roads and bridges, but also to free peasants from obligatory and onerous services so that they might better devote their time to their own land.

Harassment of peasants by their lords was an abuse vigorously opposed in many countries. Physical mistreatment, illegal expulsion of peasants from their land, and the dishonesty of patrimonial courts were practices whose incidence was considerably reduced by a much increased watchfulness on the part of royal officials, as well as by the removal or regulation of public powers of administration and justice held by private landlords. In Austria, not the least of the reasons for the reform of the structure of local government by Maria Theresa in the late 1740's was her growing concern for the lot of the peasants, while in Naples and Sicily, Charles (and later Tanucci) tried to relieve peasant tenants of their landlords' oppressive presence by attracting nobles to the royal court and by decreeing the freedom of peasants to sell their produce in the open market rather than at much depressed prices to their lords only.

The category of "social reform," however, must also include a variety of foundations for the care of widows, orphans, invalids, and the sick—which flourished in this period—as well as expanded programs of poor relief and certain kinds of social services of an almost modern nature. In many cases, the monarchical attacks on church property and on non-religious public functions of the clergy made an extension of state social welfare programs a necessity if such services were to be provided at all. Funds from the administration of confiscated church property were often earmarked by rulers for the same charitable purposes they had earlier served. The range of proposals for improvements in public assistance was limitless; among some of the most interesting actually executed were the voluntary fire-insurance plans subsidized by a number of small German states, as well as the municipal reorganizations carried out by Leopold in Florence and later in Vienna, in which police districts were provided with an attending physician and a midwife to give free assistance to victims of accidents, ill and elderly indigents, and expectant mothers. All rulers paid a much greater attention also to problems of urban lighting, sanitation, vice, and mendicancy; indeed, social "city planning" in Europe really had its origins in this period.

3 / The Interpretation of Reform

Reforms, or indeed all actions, mean nothing in themselves, of course; they gain meaning only relative to other things—the intent of the reformer, the conditions that preceded them and those that came after them, their connection with one another, and so on. The process of establishing such meaning is always an interpretative one, and must always be conducted with the facts of reform clearly in mind. While this section will treat the interpretation of reform under the same headings as those employed in the description of reform, it would be well to remember that these categories are by no means entirely separate and distinct; indeed, their very overlapping is an important conditioning factor of interpretation itself.

GOVERNMENTAL AND ADMINISTRATIVE REFORM

When Voltaire in 1765 declared that the cause of the king in France was also the cause of the *philosophes,* he was expressing a view commonly held in enlightened circles regarding the nature of the governmental and administrative reforms then underway in so many European states. Briefly stated, that view was that monarchs and ministers everywhere, to one degree or another influenced by enlightened ideas, were attempting a revision of the political framework of their states as the prelude to and the enabling act for a sweeping series of reforms that would eliminate the irrationalities and injustices of society. Specifically, there was much pleasure at what appeared to be an attempt to assert monarchical authority against the reactionary intermediate groups, especially the nobility, whose special privileges stood directly in the way of really thorough reform.

To a degree, the *philosophes* were right. Monarchs with other reforms in mind did indeed recognize administrative reorganization as a measure necessary to accommodate such reforms; they saw, too, that the strengthening of their sovereign authority against traditional corporate groups was a prerequisite for any policy that might adversely touch the self-interest of those groups. But this was nothing new. The history of monarchy in Europe since the Middle Ages had tended towards greater political unification and the ever more complete subordination of feudal intermediate authorities to the control of the crown. To that extent, the governmental reforms of the period 1760–90 form merely another chapter in the development of absolutism, regarded as the attempt to eliminate or neutralize all political competitors of the sovereign monarch.

The traditional method of doing this was the elaboration of a bureaucracy, a group of administrators at all levels, whose pay and authority came directly from the monarch, and whose loyalty therefore belonged directly to him. In the name of the king, these officials undertook to encroach upon the authority and autonomy of nobility, towns, and clergy, in the interests of reclaiming feudalized governmental functions for the monarch. The continuation of this long historical process can be seen in the reforms of this period in many countries, through the rationalization of bureaucracies, the growth in the number of their personnel, and the extension of their range of functions, some entirely new in themselves and others simply transferred to them from the hands of older, semi-public authorities (the noble estates, the guild corporations, the universities, and so on). Besides the concern for the political autonomy of the monarch that was to animate these bureaucrats were the goals of economy and increased efficiency for the whole governmental machine, for this was an age when the economic strength and the internal organization of states were being tested mightily by great international wars.

Most reforms were aimed fundamentally at greater centralization of power; the bureaucratization of the state, in other words, was a means to increase and assure the reality of the monarch's power as the sole legislator and policy-maker in his realm. In some instances, however—and here lies one of the novelties of this period—it had become clear that bureaucracies themselves could interfere with and therefore become in a sense competitors for the exercise of political authority. To explain this, it is necessary to remember that the growth of absolute power in the hands of monarchs had never followed a specific or carefully planned blueprint; on the contrary, it had everywhere been the result of a policy of expediency, of grasping opportunities for the assertion of a greater authority whenever and wherever such opportunities arose.

In France, for example, the opposition of the privileged orders to monarchical power was overcome partly by the creation of a royal bureaucracy in which commoners occupied a very important place. As time went on, the position of these commoners as royal servants was strengthened against the old feudality by granting or selling patents of nobility to them; so that, by the beginning of the eighteenth century, the Crown had in effect created a new nobility, a bureaucratic one, as a counterweight to the old. In Prussia, on the other hand, noble opposition to the growth of royal authority had been cleverly neutralized in the late seventeenth and early eighteenth centuries by a series of compromises that favored the landowning nobles against the towns in taxation, confirmed their local social and economic privileges, and guaranteed them the important positions in both army and civil service—in return, in effect, for their abdication of pretensions to political power. In many other countries, too, the process of strengthening central power had been much facilitated by the utilization of members of the old nobility as administrators in the new monarchies; by a system of inducements and rewards, which attracted some members of the nobility to the crown as its servants, the corporate unity of the nobility was broken, and with it the effectiveness of its resistance to the growth of royal authority.

On the other hand, the acquiescence of the higher orders of

society to the political sovereignty of the monarch had also been purchased by confirming various traditional exemptions and local jurisdictions and privileges, which had resulted in an often uneasy compromise between the spheres of royal and aristocratic competence. It was this compromise that, after the middle of the eighteenth century, increasingly came under attack by monarchical authority, and precisely because the terms of the compromise had become fetters on the ability of monarchs to realize their state goals. It was no mere whim, but rather the vastly increased fiscal needs of the state that precipitated a new movement towards accumulation of power at the center; for, without new power, rulers could not expect to open up one of the major sources of new revenue that had hitherto, by their own consent, been largely closed to them: the fiscal exemptions of the privileged classes, representing an immense fund of wealth.

The aristocratic character of their own bureaucracies now became a positive danger. Joseph II, lamenting the failure of so many of his reform measures, often complained that no one really understood what he was trying to do. This was perhaps true for the population as a whole. But in his own bureaucracy, the exact opposite was the case; his administrators, eager to do his will in most things, recognized all too well what he was trying to do, and they were not willing to preside over the extinction of the privileges of the aristocracy of which they were members. And in the absence of any articulate or influential body of supporters of reform, their ragdoll passivity had much to do with the tenuousness of Josephine reforms. In Prussia, the more realistic Frederick II did not attempt the direct frontal assault on privilege that Joseph so lightly took up; he cajoled and occasionally even threatened the nobility, but usually pulled up short of invading the realm of local privilege that he and his predecessors had guaranteed them. But he, too, recognized that his bureaucracy had developed autonomous potentialities, and that the aristocratic origins of its members could place it astride the paths he might wish to take. Much of the innovation that Frederick brought to the Prussian administration must therefore be seen as a deliberate attempt to disorganize and decentralize the administration, involving the circumvention of his own bureaucracy, to the end of insuring the continuation of the full integrity of royal command of the state.

Much evidence indicates that Leopold, in both Tuscany and Austria, recognized the serious deficiencies of the bureaucratized absolute state. His proposal for a constitution in Tuscany, his many attempts to involve citizens in the administration of their own affairs, and his return of power to various local and corporate groups in the Austrian monarchy after Joseph's death—all bespeak more than merely an intellectual conviction of the justice of self-government. Leopold was just as reform-minded as Joseph; but he knew that reliance on a bureaucracy alone was not enough, especially when the bureaucracy consisted largely of members of groups whose privileges were a prime target of the reforms themselves. By encouraging greater popular participation in government, Leopold hoped to educate the privileged classes to the need for reform, but also to create a wider base of positive public support for reform than his unfortunate brother had had. If Leopold had worn the crown of Austria for twenty years instead of only two, some extremely interesting political forms might have developed. As it was, only the temporizing effects of his work remained.

In France, both the inadequacy of the attention paid to bureaucratic development and reform during the eighteenth century by the central government and the combined opposition to reform of the court nobility and the "new" nobility of the *parlements* (most of whom by the mid-century had adopted the political views of the older, feudal nobility) resulted in proposals to establish a network of provincial assemblies, whose stated purpose would be that of assisting the government in provincial administration; but it was no secret that they were also intended to broaden the base of popular support for royal reform and, specifically, to give the lie to the *parlements'* false propaganda that their opposition to the royal government stemmed from their concern for the public welfare. A greater degree of independence for municipal corporations, together with the advisory work of the provincial assemblies, would then serve to strengthen the royal power against its own enemies within the government.

It should be apparent then that, in some countries, governmental reorganization designed to centralize political authority could make use of administrative decentralization to accomplish its goal. Old expediencies had come home to roost; new ones were required to correct the deficiencies of the old. In most countries, bureaucratic expansion and an increased centralization of the administrative machine were still the rule; but in all cases, efficiency, economy, and the preservation or increase of monarchical sovereignty were the primary objects of governmental reform, and only the particular situations of each country dictated the differences in the way they were achieved.

In any case, few facts justify the conclusion that the governmental reforms of the enlightened monarchs were in any way aimed at the creation of structural political forms much different from those that already existed. Representative institutions, in particular, were by-passed or suppressed in more countries than they were created or encouraged, and in any case they were always conceived as advisory and administrative aids, not as legislative bodies. The one monarch who might have made them something more—Leopold—never really had the chance to do so in Austria, and in Tuscany never quite had the nerve to introduce his famous constitution.

ECONOMIC AND FISCAL REFORM

On the surface, certain features of the economic policies of the European monarchies after 1760 appear to justify the claims of the *philosophes* in their own day that the dawn of the rule of Nature and Reason had come to economic life. A palpable increase in the general freedom of economic life, associated with various experiments in freedom of commerce, the abolition of a number of restrictions of production, and other progressive measures, seemed to provide the necessary proof that monarchs were on the point of eliminating the artificial system that had favored some sectors of the economy at the expense of others and had unnaturally restricted the increase of social wealth. The Physiocrats, in particular, congratulated themselves on their apparent influence on such monarchs as Leopold of Tuscany, Charles of Spain, Catherine of Russia, Gustavus of Sweden,

Charles Frederick of Baden, and a number of other rulers and ministers who knew their works, in some instances corresponded with them or invited them to their courts, and occasionally even attempted to carry out some of their specific theories in practice.

Again, the *philosophes* were right—to a point. It is undoubtedly true that some policies of free trade, taxation, and agricultural encouragement can be laid more or less directly at the door of Physiocratic theorists and their popularizers, whose influence on the thinking of a number of monarchs can be well documented. But it is well to remember that free-trade experiments were for the most part both tentative and temporary, that they were tried in economies whose general character was still overwhelmingly regimented, and that monarchs were always prepared at an instant's notice to revoke them—and, on occasion, did so.

Monarchs, unlike the philosophers, never looked upon freedom in the economy as an end in itself, but only as a possible means to the end of a greater increase of taxable wealth—and as a means they were perfectly willing to try out only under conditions that would not disturb the rest of the economy too much. They were also quite ready to forsake it if short-term results did not justify its continuance. The regulation or suppression of the guilds, hailed by many enlightened spirits as evidence of the devotion of rulers to the principle of freedom, was in fact undertaken only after solid evidence had demonstrated that guild privileges contributed substantially to restrict production and therefore to reduce potential tax revenues. In other respects, governments continued to protect and favor certain industries over others, according to their estimation of their final contribution to the state treasury, and showed no interest in the principle of equality of treatment of all merchants and manufacturers as individuals, which they were sometimes credited with by admiring *philosophes;* the individual received treatment in rough accordance with the state's evaluation of his economic contribution to it.

The greatly increased interest in agriculture characteristic of governments in the 1760's and 1770's has sometimes been ascribed to the influence of the Physiocrats, who valued the extractive industries above all others and who constantly complained about the favoritism shown by governments to industry rather than agriculture. Probably it is more accurate to say that some of the directions of agricultural reform were shaped to some extent by Physiocratic ideas; the *interest* in agricultural improvement, however, came from a general problem known to Physiocrats and governments alike—a steady rise in the price of foodstuffs all over Europe since the 1730's, reflecting the heavier demands of a rapidly increasing population on a more or less static production. An increase in the prices of agricultural commodities inevitably raised wage levels, which in turn raised the price of manufactured goods and placed the country where they were produced at a disadvantage in international competition. Furthermore, any grain shortages, no matter how temporary, raised to rulers' minds the specter of famine, bread riots, and other disturbing social dislocations.

Thus, at precisely the time when rulers were seeking means to increase agricultural production, the Physiocrats, working on the problem from a different angle, appeared on the scene with doctrines that promised not only to solve the problem of shortage, but also to increase the general economic tempo of society by enlarging internal markets through securing greater prosperity— and therefore also greater buying power—for the huge mass of agricultural producers. Even at that, however, Physiocratic experiments did not last very long where they were tried at all; nor did rulers see agricultural improvement in any very theoretical terms: it was necessary in order to assure the continued growth of manufactures, to be sure, but it was always the manufactures that came first in their plans. A general amelioration of production resulted in this period, but it occurred under the eclectic supervision of monarchs who were far too practical to turn their states into experimental laboratories for Physiocratic theorists.

The widespread reform of fiscal systems, connected also with administrative reorganization, was very deliberately aimed at the maximization of revenues through increased efficiency, decreased costs of collection, and the rationalization of tax systems (in the sense of adjusting the tax burden so that it would act as little to deter economic growth as possible). Confiscations of church property, as well as frequent attempts to introduce increased taxation of both clergy and nobility, must be seen in the context of governmental desire to liberate the "dead" wealth represented by clerical and aristocratic property, not as an attempt to assert the equality of property irrespective of the proprietor's class.

To aristocrats as well as commoners, and of course to the *philosophes,* it sometimes appeared that the abolition of certain exemptions for the privileged classes had the character of an assault on privilege itself. In certain respects, such was indeed the effect. But confiscation and taxation were only two methods of increasing the circulation and investment of capital; and, in reality, they were not always the most important. By the preferred method of encouraging nobles to invest in their land through the erection of credit institutions for their use, by the creation of state banks to encourage saving for ultimate investment, and, in a few cases, even by modifying strict rules against the participation of aristocrats in business and commercial pursuits, monarchs sought to accomplish their economic goal short of invading aristocratic proprietary privilege. Only when these measures did not seem adequate—and when the bourgeoisie and peasantry simply could not carry any more fiscal burdens without their destruction as taxable objects—were steps taken to pry wealth out of the hands of the fiscally privileged. The conclusion is inescapable that for most rulers the reduction of privilege in this case was more an unpleasant necessity than a desired goal.

It is probably true that governments of this period demonstrated a greater sense of responsibility in the management of economic and fiscal affairs than had many of their predecessors; but this was more a result of increased need and greater sophistication, perhaps, than of an improved conscience. A constantly growing fund of knowledge and experience in economic affairs, together with greater reliance on statistics and accurate surveys and the imitation of successful foreign institutions (such as the English banking and commercial system), resulted in sounder policies almost everywhere. But planning and control extended even to economic freedom; and social utility, as defined by the ruler for his state, rather than individual benefit remained as it had been for more than a century, the unshakeable foundation of absolutistic economic policy.

RELIGIOUS REFORM

Probably no other series of reforms produced as much jubilation among the *philosophes* and their disciples, or as much conviction of the good intentions of the enlightened princes under whose rule they had the good fortune to live, than those that pertained to religion and the organized churches. In both Protestant and Catholic countries, the rapid progress of toleration brought evidence that monarchs, at least, had finally perceived the stupidity of persecutions based on differences of opinion about matters where objective knowledge was impossible, and were thus moving to eliminate religious belief as a criterion of citizenship and civic loyalty.

On this point, princes and philosophers were indeed in agreement, but the former did not always share the latter's great enthusiasm for religious free-thinking, since with a few exceptions—e.g., Frederick II—they retained at least a semblance of, and sometimes a deep and sincere belief in, their own orthodox confessions, whether Protestant or Catholic. But even many of the *philosophes* concurred with princes who believed in at least the provisional social necessity of the organized churches as a moral deterrent to crime and disorder, as Voltaire's famous aphorism might indicate: "Philosophy for the classes, religion for the masses." Toleration, of course, had its practical side, too, for intolerance bred social antagonisms and conflicts that could be politically dangerous and economically disastrous. The expulsion of the Protestant Huguenots from France by Louis XIV in 1685 was still frequently cited elsewhere in Europe as an example of how intolerance could damage the economy of a state, since many of the Huguenots were skilled artisans and businessmen whose absorption into the economies of other states (Prussia and Holland, for example) was of great benefit to those countries. In a number of respects, then, toleration was a principle as useful to states as it was just to philosophy; and, even in the countries of Catholic Europe, or in Sweden where public opinion was anything but congenial to it, it was often practiced by governments even if it could not be very loudly preached.

State intervention, regulation, and control of church affairs, commonly regarded in the enlightened community as a laudable attempt to limit the social influence of a vicious and obscurantist priestcraft that had entrenched itself behind walls of wealth and privilege, was in fact a phenomenon with profound political and economic motivations. Politically, it represents a major stage in the centuries-long conflict between the church and the state over the question of their respective spheres of authority—the spiritual and the temporal. In the course of the Reformation, most Protestant confessions, partly from conviction and partly from necessity, had been content to allow the state to define rather narrowly the sphere of spiritual power, eliminating from the church such important rights as ownership of property, organization of its officers as a distinct social order or estate, and autonomy with respect to its internal administration. In Catholic countries, some similar developments had taken place, but to a much lesser degree, because monarchs in these countries were satisfied to permit a great deal of independence and social and economic prestige to the Church as long as it provided moral—and a certain measure of material—support for the state and did not compete with the monarch for authority in a well-defined sphere where the state was to be supreme.

But by the late eighteenth century, it had become impossible to reconcile this arrangement of mutual deference and support with the implications of the new tasks and policies the state had set out for itself. The economic element was certainly of great importance here; one aspect of this, the confiscation of church property and the reduction of ecclesiastical tax exemptions, has already been discussed. In other respects, too, however, the Church presented obstacles to the realization of economies held to be important by the state. Large sums of money spent on rituals, ceremonies, and processions, for example, were often regarded as wholly wasteful extravagances that consumed money badly needed elsewhere in the economy without giving any benefit, even a spiritual one, in return. Similarly, excessive holidays were held to waste productive labor. Furthermore, church tithing, carried on independent of the state, represented virtually a public tax in Catholic countries; as such, and given the much increased interest of the state in all economic and fiscal matters that touched the generality of their subjects, it was entirely natural that princes would regard it as a part of their prerogative to investigate and regulate church income and expenditure and to recommend or impose such changes on the administration of ecclesiastical finances as they deemed necessary to insure both the integrity of the Church's mission in the world and the welfare of secular society.

In effect, then, the state now attempted to assume a control function over the Catholic church greatly exceeding what had previously existed. Limitation of the activity of church tribunals and administrative bodies, supervision of public utterances and pastoral letters of bishops, heightened interference in the appointment of the higher clergy, and stricter regulation of communications with Rome were all part of a general movement to alter and restrict the very definition of the scope of the Church's function in public life. In some cases, the educational functions of the Church were reduced. At the same time, however, a deliberate effort was made to enlist the energies of the secular clergy as servants of the public welfare as defined by the state; to this end, the education of priests was declared to be a matter of state concern, as was the curriculum they taught in the schools. In this way, both the lectern and the pulpit were "tuned" to serve the secular goals of civic morality and economic diligence. The monastic clergy, of course, except those who in effect already served a public function (nursing and teaching), were regarded as pure parasites whose numbers ought to be reduced.

These changes were no mere adjustment of relationships to guarantee the political sovereignty of the ruler, but an entirely new chapter in church-state relations, at least in the Catholic countries. They were an attempt to subject the Church to scrutiny as a secular organization that, like any other institution with important social functions and effects, therefore lay within the regulative power of the state, at least with respect to its public and secular characteristics. It was clear that the Church and its officers would retain certain privileges for a long time to come; but the more or less successful assertion of the principle that the state had the right and duty to supervise all societal aspects of the ecclesiastical establishment represents not only an important step in the maturation of the idea of the state as superior to all private corporations whatsoever, but also a significant stage in the progress of secular philosophies of society.

LEGAL AND JUDICIAL REFORM

For the average *philosophe,* the word "law" was almost sacred; it symbolized the objective order of the physical universe, it was the manifestation of human reason in its governance of human society, and in it lay all the difference between legitimate government and tyranny. Good laws, well administered—or at the very least the absence of bad laws—were the keys to well-being; and certainly the widespread reform of law and legal systems in this period gave the publicists of the Enlightenment good reason to believe that the various crowned heads of Europe had discovered those keys and were beginning to use them. They also had some basis for believing that their own works and insights played some part in the reform then underway. Catherine II, for example, had copied material wholesale from Montesquieu's *Spirit of the Laws* in her *Instruction* of 1767 and had conferred either in person or by correspondence with leading French *philosophes* on the subject of law; the works of Cesare Beccaria were known and cited in every court in Europe, and the man himself was called to advise the Austrian government by Leopold II in 1791. Furthermore, the preambles of revised law codes, the reports of legal commissions, and the content of many legal reform decrees not infrequently utilized phrases and ideas from eighteenth-century philosophic tracts.

But, in spite of the debt that many rulers cheerfully acknowledged to the *philosophes,* it is highly doubtful that their reforms were to any very considerable degree directly attributable to the influence of philosophic persuasion. In matters of law and justice, as elsewhere, there were compelling practical reasons for a thorough review of law and its implementation in reform. For one thing, increased efficiency meant money saved; and whether this was applied to reorganization of the court system, to the shortening of court procedure, to improvement of the quality of judges (which also tended to shorten procedure), or compilation and unification of laws, both the state and the citizen benefitted from it economically. Lawsuits were as common and numerous in that day as in this, and in all strata of the population, including the peasantry—among whom, the eighteenth-century equivalent of "ambulance-chasing" was practiced by shady lawyers who, searching for new fees, actively encouraged peasants to hop off to court at the slightest provocation, regardless of the merits of their case. Incompetent judges, lengthy written procedures, and unclear and conflicting laws were only a few of the abuses that rendered litigation a drain on the time and the finances of both officials and litigants, and which provided reasons enough in themselves for reform. Similarly, the separation of judicial from administrative organs allowed both to function better and at smaller cost to the state.

Nor should it be forgotten that, for all the undoubtedly genuine humanitarian concerns of many rulers, their readiness to reform penal laws was much increased by the material benefits that the state might derive from it. This was perhaps not so true for the abolition of torture, whose results, in the form of confessions and the naming of accomplices, were simply recognized as untrustworthy, but was a major factor in the elimination or restriction of the use of maiming and capital punishment. When Joseph II restricted the imposition of capital punishment, to use one example, he termed it too mild a penalty for the most serious crimes, as well as a useless squandering of labor; for it, he substituted lifetime penal labor, whose economic benefits for the state were obvious. Maiming, similarly, merely made a potential beggar out of an able-bodied worker. Thus, what is often forgotten in the discussion of penal reform in the eighteenth century is that, while many penalties for crime were changed, they usually remained harsh and frequently involved hard labor in prison-workhouses, which were in effect state factories where the criminal was not merely punished but also put to work to increase social production.

One major political motive for legal reform, which has already been mentioned elsewhere, had to do with the still incomplete character of the eighteenth-century dynastic-territorial state. The imposition of a single, unified law code applicable to all the territories that had heretofore operated under the separate legal systems that they had brought into the state as they were absorbed into it at different times was as important a step in bringing about the political unity of the state as was the creation of a single army or a uniform administrative system, both of which had been realized a good deal earlier in most countries. Army and administration were, of course, of greater importance to the basic security of the state than was the legal system, and it was therefore natural that more attention was paid to them at a much earlier date. But in the long run, the unity of the modern state also required a uniformity of its laws.

It might be suggested, too, that another and more subtle political motive for extensive codification and unification of law lay in the desire to make the law more of a positive administrative support for monarchical authority and policy than it had been before. The volume of state business in the late eighteenth century, especially in view of the added tasks brought by reforms themselves, was much greater than it had ever been before. In all countries, bureaucracies were expanded to handle this increased business; but even bureaucracies required a constant standard to make daily decisions; without it, the burden of decision-making at the center would be as great as ever, and the monarch himself overwhelmed with a vast and growing mass of detail. Law itself—uniform, clear, and simple—could provide such a standard, for its provisions would represent the exact will of the sovereign and an infallible and obligatory guide to action for his officials.

Thus, in the face of rapidly increasing state business that simply exceeded the command of any single individual and with a troubled awareness of the autonomous tendencies of their own bureaucracies, rulers began to see law as an indispensable helpmeet in the work of government and administration. All of them had indeed become "first servants of the state," as Frederick II

was fond of putting it. This was not only a philosophy of rulership, but also an expression of the cold, hard fact that the state
had become bigger than the ruler. Monarchs were forced therefore by their own desire to remain absolute to an acceptance of
a kind of rule of law. The direction they took in their codifications demonstrates a tendency to combine the general principles
of law and a philosophy of government, together with civil,
criminal, and administrative law, into a single code or interlock-
ing set of codes. The most successful of these, the Prussian code
of 1794, is in some respects almost a written constitution for the
Prussian state. Such written instruments were valuable, then, for
they at once preserved the integrity of monarchical rule and
guaranteed a regularity of administration without the constant
detailed attention of the already overtaxed personal energies of
the monarch.

Again, it was Frederick II who wrote that "Only the laws
must rule. The duty of the ruler is restricted to protecting them."
And Frederick, together with other monarchs of his time, made
sincere efforts to implement this belief by separating administrative and judicial organs more carefully and by limiting their own
interference in the courts. There were, of course, instances where
they felt these judicial organs of the state to be failing in their
duty, thus requiring corrective action from the sovereign who was,
after all, the only authority capable of doing it. It is this principle
that explains Frederick's famous intervention in the case of the
miller Arnold, a peasant who received an unfavorable judgment
in litigation with a noble. Frederick wrongly believed the verdict
ascribable to aristocratic prejudice on the part of the judges. The
fact of the king's interference, together with his extraordinarily
harsh treatment of the judges, created a stir all over Europe and
temporarily darkened his enlightened reputation. But it became
a *cause célèbre*, of course, precisely because it was an unusual
stain on an otherwise bright record. Still, these attempts by
princes to establish the self-sufficiency of the law cannot be regarded as an acceptance of a real limitation of their own sovereignty; they were designed, on the contrary, to augment it. It
was the princes who continued to make the law, after all, and

who intended to benefit from the greater freedom permitted them by institutionalizing their commands in a clear and rational body of law.

In general, it is not possible to speak of any major changes in the substance of civil or criminal law during this period except, as noted, in penal codes. Equality in the application of law was more earnestly solicited than in earlier periods, perhaps; but, in the still hierarchical social order of the European states, there remained numerous areas where the content of the law itself was unequal, i.e., where the law was differently written for different classes of men. Only in a very restricted sense, therefore, was "equality before the law" advanced in practice by the work of legal reform in this period. On the other hand, of course, inasmuch as law was itself a tool of reform in other aspects of the monarchs' work, the principle of equality could be and occasionally was used to justify the right of the state to invade some area of privilege—church property, for example. But it was too dangerous a principle to be insisted upon too often or too loudly and therefore was employed with great circumspection.

EDUCATIONAL REFORM

In its broadest sense, "education" was one of the most cherished parts of the public program of the Enlightenment; it was, after all, the means whereby the insights and attitudes that made up the philosophy of the Enlightenment were to be spread throughout society and made effective. The tolerance for ideas that the *philosophes* so insistently demanded was really nothing more or less than the freedom to persuade and convert society to their own rationality. It is therefore not surprising that they looked with approval on the policy of governments that in this period encouraged publication and dissemination of some kinds of enlightened tracts, expanded the freedom of the press, supported the activities of private learned societies, and, finally, began to pay some real attention to the question of popular schooling.

A closer look at these government policies will reveal, however, that monarchs' conceptions of popular enlightenment differed in some important respects from those of the *philosophes*. Most important, rulers knew how to differentiate between those ideas that were useful to them and those that were not and how to propagate the former without encouraging the latter. In all countries, the interest of governments was consistently greatest in the propagation of technical and vocational knowledge. Their encouragement of publications, for the most part, was limited to books and journals that discussed such socially uncontroversial subjects as mechanics, industrial management, agriculture, animal husbandry, and economic, fiscal, and administrative technology. Similarly, the various public and private academies and societies that they supported were concerned mostly with the dissemination of new tools and techniques of potential importance to the economy of the country; an examination of the topics offered by these groups as subjects for prize essays, for example, will reveal a rather one-sided preoccupation with practical advancements in industry and, above all, in agriculture.

Changes sponsored by governments in the curricula of universities and seminaries demonstrate a comparable emphasis on preparing students for teaching or for one or another aspect of government administrative work that involved less literary or classical knowledge and more vocational and practical knowledge. The curricula of new systems of public education, especially among the peasantry, were also dominated by attempts to improve the conditions of life and labor of the lower classes and were designed ultimately to increase their economic productivity and their utilization of their own resources. At the same time, even with the greatly increased domination of the state in educational affairs, religious instruction was retained to provide a moral background for new attempts to teach a kind of civic responsibility, in which the individual child was to be taught the necessity of law and order, the purpose of government, and his own importance as a contributor to the welfare of society.

Much of what the twentieth century thinks of as the "Philosophy of the Enlightenment"—namely, the social criticism of such leading figures as Voltaire, Diderot, Rousseau, and so on—found very little place in the social education sponsored by governments. It is true that specific criticisms, especially those regarding the social and economic position of the clergy or the stupidity and inhumanity of serfdom, could be and actually were used by rulers as instruments to support specific reform policies. But this did not necessarily imply acceptance of the philosophy behind the criticism; and rulers continued almost everywhere to employ censorship to exclude or minimize the influence of many new doctrines, especially political ones, on the populace as a whole.

In the final analysis, then, the economic or fiscal motivation of governments was as strong in their educational policies as it was in any other category of reform. And it is this, of course, that explains the uniformly heavy interest in developing useful technical and vocational skills among the people, from the sons of peasants to the sons of aristocrats, and not excluding girls, whose education now also began to be considered in terms of its possible social utility. The same rather narrow practicality also explains the attitudes of monarchs such as Frederick II, who at one time questioned the utility of teaching even reading and writing to peasants on the grounds of the possibility that, once outfitted with these skills, far from becoming better farmers, they might be tempted to desert agriculture entirely and flock to the cities to become "clerks and such things."

It is quite clear also that many of the educational schemes considered or adopted by governments in this period were related to a deep insight among rulers and their advisors about the difficulty of carrying out reforms successfully in societies too ignorant to understand the nature and purpose of the reforms. The history of much reform in this and earlier periods demonstrates that the inability of rulers to develop popular support for their programs, even among groups that would benefit substantially from them, was a major factor in the failure of reform; and it was ignorance that was finally to blame. In view of the opposition their programs awakened among groups whose privileges would be lessened by reform, as well as of the passivity or hostility of their own bureaucracies, rulers increasingly recognized the need to awaken some popular energies, some popular voluntarism, in favor of reform. Without it, they stood very nearly alone; and it exceeded the capacities of even the most energetic princes to impose permanent innovation single-handed on societies the size of theirs. Joseph II proved that well enough. Education was therefore a desperately needed political tool among absolute monarchs who had begun to realize the real limitations of their absolutism.

SOCIAL REFORM

Among the numerous features of the Old Regime in Europe that seemed to the enlightened community inconsistent with the principles of a rational society, none was regarded with greater loathing than serfdom. More than any other institution, hereditary servitude symbolized the groundless legal inequities that so confused and oppressed public life, and which prevented individuals from making their best contribution to society. When, in the decades after 1760, monarchs began or once again picked up the threads of agrarian reform, it was entirely commensurate with their view of their own society that many *philosophes* should regard the rulers' activity as an attack on inequality and its adverse effects on society.

In fact, neither the character nor the effects of peasant reform can justify the conclusion that the inequality of the peasant was, in itself, a matter of much concern to monarchs and their governments. A variety of statements from princes and their ministers can be cited to demonstrate a sympathy with the plight of the peasants and a willingness to ameliorate their situation. But the number of states where serfdom, where it existed at all, was directly attacked by governments was not large; and in a few cases, as in Russia, the realm of servitude was actually extended.

What was of concern to the governments of this time, however, was that the peasantry and their economic viability be secured against whatever forces might threaten them. In some countries, Prussia affording the best (but not the only) example, the large peasantry provided the common soldiers for the army; everywhere, their ranks provided the complete and necessary labor for placing waste land under new cultivation. For these and other reasons, it was necessary for the state to intervene in the landlord-peasant relationship to prevent mistreatment of peasants or their expulsion from their tenures. At the same time, the extraordinary burdens in services, dues, and taxes under which the peasant labored made it financially difficult for him to improve his land, while his uncertain tenure, lack of a written contract specifying his rents and fees, and other factors made it wholly uncertain that he or his descendants would reap the benefits of any improvements he might make. As long as these conditions existed, agricultural advancement at the lowest and quantitatively most important level was impossible.

When rulers then stepped in to lower taxes, to grant tax remissions in bad years, to press for written contracts between peasants and their lords, to grant or recommend hereditary tenure of land and the commutation of labor services into cash payments, and so forth, they were seeking to protect and ameliorate the peasantry *as a class*, not as individuals whose rights had to be made equal to those of other classes. The fact is that their rights were not equal to those of other classes, and no ruler attempted to perpetrate the fiction that they were. The motivation for the increased protection afforded to this class of producers was again related directly to the concrete military and economic needs of the state. To be sure, it was easy to mistake these measures for an attack on the principle of serfdom, since some of the ties of personal dependency between lord and peasant that were a part of the serf's status were attacked as a virtually unavoidable part of the method of accomplishing the more general goal. Since it was unavoidable, governments sometimes justified their measures by reference to the inhumanity or injustice of serfdom and occasionally went so far as to suggest its utter abolition.

But patrimonial privileges were not generally attacked past the point where the state's economic interest stopped, except in cases such as Denmark-Norway, where peasants' situations were already so favorable that complete abolition of servitude represented only a minor loss to lords, a loss usually made up by other compensation. The hesitancy of monarchs to invade the patrimonial sphere very deeply was also directly related to their continued dependence on the upper landowning classes for experienced personnel in both the military and the civil administration. A real assault on their patrimonial rights, which constituted the last and in many ways the most important body of their privileges, would have called forth an opposition whose violence, in countries such as Prussia or Russia, conceivably could have resulted in a disastrous disorganization of the military establishment and the collapse of local and provincial government. The agrarian reforms of Joseph II, who had made up his mind to the necessity of removing the landlord as a buffer between the state and the peasantry, constituted an exception to the caution of rulers dealing with the gentry in such matters. The results of his reforms provide proof of the wisdom of caution under then-existing circumstances.

The other part of "social reform"—the considerably increased state interest in institutions for the care of the socially distressed —perfectly demonstrates the coincidence of humanitarian or charitable and utilitarian motivations. Obviously, both Christian and humanistic sentiments dictated that the poor and indigent not be allowed to starve. On the other hand, there was no reason why the able-bodied—whether beggars, orphans, or widows, adults or (to a point) children—should not earn their keep, especially since in doing so they might learn a trade and thus be provided with the opportunity of becoming useful citizens instead of wards of the state. Many public institutions for the care of such people therefore took on the character of educational workhouses, which satisfied the demands of charity and contributed to fill the labor needs of industry and manufacturing.

CONCLUSION

Any summary and general evaluation of the great reform movements that characterized the last few decades of the eighteenth century before the French Revolution must conclude that, while the humanitarian sincerity and social benevolence of many of the leading monarchs and statesmen of this period can hardly be doubted, cold political and economic requirements of their states and their thrones had the ultimate voice in determining both the specific character of the reforms undertaken and the limits of their own reform goals.

But we should remember, too, how much of the total reform

work of this period in all categories was a legacy from the past, especially of the problem of establishing basic political unity within the various states of Europe, a problem that had plagued monarchs since the end of the middle ages. As we have mentioned elsewhere, nearly all of the states discussed were to one degree or another still incomplete states, ones whose uneven growth over a period of hundreds of years presented even in 1760 a picture of a bewildering variety of internal differences. Austria is perhaps the best example of a state whose internal integration and unity were in this period still at a very low level; but Prussia, Russia, and others show many of the same characteristics. In this sense, the striving of monarchs to increase their sovereignty, which along the way involved the suppression of local and corporate rights and privileges, was also a necessary part of the movement towards political integration and unification that has characterized the growth of all modern states since feudal times.

In any case, the strength and unity of the state as a military-economic unit and the preservation of the political integrity of monarchical absolutism were the fundamental goals of all the rulers of major states, who had to contend with the ever-present menace of war in a rather unpredictable international climate; lesser monarchs, unable or unwilling to compete in the power struggles that did so much to shape the policy of the larger states, still accepted the challenges posed by economic and political problems in order to strengthen their rule and tidy up the obvious irrationalities of their states. Certainly it is possible to maintain that pure benevolence and a concern for the rights and welfare of individuals appeared more often in the smaller states with "reforming" princes (and not all of them did, by any means) than in the greater monarchies, where the welfare of the state, not of the individual or the group, was sought.

These two welfares were not by any means the same thing. In the numerous letters, papers, and political testaments of the monarchs who professed themselves enlightened, the term "welfare" or an equivalent is used to cover as wide a variety of concerns as the reforms of the period themselves covered; but its primary meaning is nearly always "security," and that, in turn,

was invariably applied first to the state, and therefore meant defense against foreign powers. Any measures that might strengthen the economy ("Money is the sinews of war"), increase revenues, make the administration more efficient, or increase the ability of the people themselves to make contributions to a stronger state were subject to consideration for adoption. At the same time, however, the limits to the amount and kind of reform that could be carried out were mostly drawn by rulers themselves, for they instinctively recognized that too considerable or rapid a change in any important aspect of traditional social life was likely to create tensions and disorders that could themselves pose great dangers for the security of the state. Joseph II's reforms and the extremely serious revolts they brought about in the Netherlands and in Hungary proved such fears to be anything but illusory. Ultimately, then, state security was both the cause and the limiting factor of reform.

This being so, it was natural that the greatest energy of monarchs was expended on reforms that were most directly related to questions of security, such as governmental-administrative and economic matters, and that those aspects of reform less obviously important to the organization of power—education, justice, social welfare in the caritative sense of the term, and so on—generally were pushed less vigorously and if necessary abandoned much sooner than the others. Also, it is quite apparent that the most successful reforms of this period came in those areas of activity where the monarch already had the greatest amount of undisputed authority, i.e., in his own administration and bureaucracy, on his own crown lands, and so forth. Wherever policies implying an actual increase of monarchical authority, or its extension to new areas of social life, were undertaken, opposition from various sources came quickly to bear on them and almost invariably forced either their abandonment or their dilution.

Since it was primarily the grim realities of eighteenth-century politics and statecraft that conditioned this long reform period, it is entirely apropos to ask why both rulers and *philosophes* apparently so often fell into the dream-world of a thing called "Enlightened Despotism"—why, that is, there was so much talk of the success of philosophy in bringing about the political rule of a rational and benevolent humanitarianism. Were men too stupid or deceived to recognize the real limits of the influence of ideas on the reforms that were taking place around them? This is an intriguing problem, but one with possible answers at several levels.

In the first place, the motives of human action are much less easy to distill and separate from their actual interconnection in the minds of living men than we sometimes like to think; and since there is much reason to affirm the sincerity of the personal enlightenment and benevolence of many rulers, it is not difficult to understand their own conviction that, within the limits of the possible, they actually were doing their best to improve the lot of their subjects according to high philosophic ideals. Furthermore, it speaks for at least the ethical influence of the Enlightenment that rulers felt a desire to justify many of their reforms in terms of enlightened ideas—that they felt their status and reputation somehow enhanced by the ascription of their reforms to humanitarian motives. This status-seeking was shared by the *philosophes*, who, like most literary men, were immensely flattered by the attention paid to them and their works by heads of state, and who were therefore only too eager to find the reasons for many of the changes effected by rulers in their own influence on them. Both princes and philosophers, then, had personal and in a sense also political reasons to emphasize the enlightened motivation of reform.

Even more important, however, is the frequently ignored fact that there was, to a point, a great deal of similarity between the reforms solicited by the *philosophes* as implications of their social criticisms and the reforms actually proposed or carried out for political reasons by the monarchs. Quite irrespective of the motivation that produced reforms, their effects in many cases tended towards the relief of abuses that the *philosophes* criticized. Thus, they could with good reason praise the activities of reforming monarchs without being accused of self-deception or impractical idealism. Clearly, reform did not in practice go as far as many of them wished; but it moved in directions they approved; and, if it did not tend towards revolution, neither, after all, did their doctrines. Nor was it a source of dismay to the proponents of enlightenment that many of the reforms they suggested for largely humanitarian reasons—penal reform, for example—were adopted in practice mainly because of their utilitarian value. To them, in fact, it was the final proof of the truth of their teachings that what was just, in absolute terms, was also useful; indeed, the enthusiasm of the *philosophes* and their almost obtuse self-confidence are scarcely comprehensible unless we remember how nearly coextensive for them were the words "Truth" and "Utility." From their standpoint, "enlightened despotism" was therefore in many respects an accurate designation for the tendencies, if not always for the motivations, of this period of reform.

Finally, we must remember that one meaning of "enlightenment" as used in the eighteenth century referred to the ability of the individual to recognize his own self-interest and to pursue it rationally, i.e., by a logical program that utilized means appropriate to his goal. In this sense, monarchy had never been so enlightened as it was in this period. Dogmas, systems, prejudices, and even tradition itself were subjected to a rational and empirical scrutiny, and they were judged according to the single standard of their contribution to the state (as that was defined by the ruler) more than had ever been the case before. A mixture of empiricism, utility, practicality, tolerance, secularism, and experimentation formed a kind of general climate that permeated courts and governments, politics and economics, social polity and intellectual life to a greater degree than ever before. It was above all the strength of this climate, or spirit, which was centuries in the making, which gave to monarchy in this period its enlightened characteristic; for just as the evolution of a new mental climate had eventuated in the eighteenth-century *philosophes'* conception of reason, so had it also produced the eighteenth-century monarchs' conception of reason-of-state. And the princes were no less adept at applying this reason to the solution of the problems of the state than were the philosophers in using theirs to solve the problems of man and the universe.

4 / Enlightened Despotism as an Epoch of European History

While it is quite apparent that the period of enlightened despotism can best be understood as one of generalized reform designed to strengthen the state and to bolster monarchical authority within the state, such a characterization is not in itself adequate to justify the designation of this period as an historically unique or distinct one. Similar reform periods, with approximately the same goals, had occurred at frequent intervals in the history of the modern state and in the history of absolute monarchy; why, then, is this period different?

It is not reform itself, but rather the universality of reform, first of all, that makes it unique—the simultaneous occurrence of reform programs throughout nearly all the states of Europe. And underneath this universal reform was an almost universal problem. Two great "world wars" in the eighteenth century—the War of the Austrian Succession from 1740 to 1748 and the Seven Years' War from 1756 to 1763, the second vastly more expensive than the first—had introduced profound crises in the affairs of government everywhere in Europe. These were partly military in nature, inasmuch as the most immediate demands of warfare always related to troops, armaments, and supplies; but the administration of the state very quickly became involved also, as it became apparent that military preparedness was as much a function of the overall efficiency of all the operations of government as it was of the efficiency of the armed forces alone. But the greatest crisis was undoubtedly the financial one, which may be expressed very simply as the inadequacy of traditional sources of revenue to meet the staggering costs of "modern" warfare in the eighteenth century.

As nearly as anything can, these crises help to explain and also to date the beginnings of enlightened despotism as a reform period. As early as the 1740's, nearly every one of the belligerents of the War of the Austrian Succession began reforms intended to remedy the weaknesses of their states that had become so evident under the pressures of military emergency. Austria in particular, but also Prussia and even France, came out of that war with an increased wisdom and with proposals for self-strengthening that they had every intention of attempting to apply. But before these were completely implemented, the Seven Years' War had begun, thus halting the slow progress of revival. By the time it was over, the financial problems not only of the belligerents but also of many non-belligerents whose economies had been affected by the war were much more serious than they had been in 1748.

Now, therefore, in the long period of peace that followed 1763, began the most intensive and comprehensive series of reforms, which in most places had the double character of a reconstruction and a preparation for the possibility of renewed war. Never had the increase of state revenues been a subject of so much investigation and concern; never had a greater rational calculation been applied to the subject; and never had the results of such calculation produced policies so comprehensive in their application to every facet of public life. The great similarity in the approaches taken to this general problem among the various states after 1763 goes back not merely to the similarities of the problem itself, nor yet only to the common characteristics of the institutions that already existed in these countries, but also to a deliberate policy of imitation produced by emergency. In this sense, it is possible to speak of this period as a major stage in the "westernization" or "modernization" of the more backward countries, especially Austria and Russia, whose now full-scale involvement in continental politics taught them the necessity of emulating the internal policies of the more efficient states of western Europe.

It is interesting to note in this connection that Catherine II tried to create municipal corporations and an hierarchical structure of nobility in Russia precisely because she was convinced that they followed a western, and therefore a more modern, pattern. Similarly, many of Maria Theresa's administrative reforms, and to some extent those of Joseph II also (who for a long time was a great admirer of Frederick II), were consciously modelled after the structures and procedures that had proved so successful for her Prussian arch-enemy. Nor are these the only examples of imitation, which can be confirmed in Prussia, Spain, and elsewhere. This sometimes occurred even within the confines of the same state; in Austria, many of Joseph's activities had the character of an attempt to bring the more backward peripheral areas of the Crown, such as Hungary, up to the greater standards of efficiency and modernity which had been achieved in Austria and Bohemia. His imposition of German as the official language of the empire was a part of this. In certain respects, therefore, enlightened despotism produced a greater uniformity in the overall characteristics of the states of Europe than had previously existed.

But, as we have intimated elsewhere, the financial crisis of the mid-century also precipitated a political crisis. The vast governmental reorganizations and the social intervention dictated by the search for new revenues and a greater degree of social organization in general posed new demands on executive and legislative authority, for which neither the theory nor the practical capabilities of traditional absolute monarchy were adequate. The fundamentals of the problem were simple: neither the administrative apparatus of the state nor the theory of the state and the monarch's place in it were sufficiently developed to permit the degree of organization and exploitation of social resources required to meet the demands of international existence and competition in the eighteenth-century states-system. One should not be deceived by the "polite" character of warfare in the eighteenth century into a belief that it consisted merely of frivolous games and exercises.

International decisions of great importance were achieved through war in this century; and, though fanaticism and ideology were largely absent from it, hard-headed realism was not. War was a matter of great and crucial concern to rulers; it was expensive and demanding and became more so as the century wore on. Only through an increasingly thorough coordination of social resources could rulers hope to measure up to the actual or anticipated challenges of international competition.

In one sense, therefore, the whole history of reform in this period is merely the story of the attempt to strengthen the state for its increased international tasks of aggression and defense. But the sheer enormity of the task that princes now undertook, combined with the formal limitations of their own hierarchical and corporative societies, posed a practical problem that they tried to solve in various ways. In some countries, an intensified development of centralized administration took place, which involved expansion of bureaucracies and a greater reliance on them; such was the basic pattern of Spain under Charles III and of Austria under Maria Theresa and Joseph II. In others, where monarchs had the insight that bureaucracy itself had become an actual or potential hindrance to reform, or where specific advantages could be gained by utilizing expert local opinion, a tendency towards some administrative decentralization can be seen. In almost all countries, furthermore, the compelling need for economic and technical expertise led to a new program of recruitment of educated middle-class advisors and administrators, the effect of which was to give a somewhat more bourgeois tone to government as well as to emphasize that merit, or the ability to perform the increasingly specialized tasks of government, was now of greater social utility than birth or social status alone.

Besides the practical problem of the mechanics of increased government intervention and control of society, however, there was also the theoretical problem of justifying such intervention and control. Too often we ignore the fact that any more or less permanent form of government rests on at least the passive consent of the socially important classes of the society. This statement is as true of absolute monarchy in the eighteenth century as it is of democracy in the twentieth century. A brief look at the theoretical foundations of absolute monarchy will help to make clear just what kind of social consent was given to this form of government, historically, and why it was given.

The growth of absolute monarchy almost everywhere rested upon a double theoretical appeal; one was religious and philosophical, the other utilitarian and practical. In the seventeenth century, to provide a convenient example, a more or less standard religious justification for sovereign monarchical authority was given by Bishop Bossuet in France, who emphasized an analogy between God the Father, who ruled all of creation absolutely, and the king who therefore ought to rule his realm absolutely. Man, tainted with original sin, always tended towards evil and malice; and it was the function of the king, who was the lieutenant of God on earth, aided by the Church, to prevent him from doing harm and bringing disorder to himself and to others, and to lead him towards the path of good.

The general tendency of this religious argument to support the unity and absolutism of royal power was reinforced by the adherents of the philosophy of Descartes, who held that there was no objectively discernible order in the universe—i.e., that no external evidence could be used to demonstrate one—and that all government was an artifice, a creation of human reason to give structure to human social life. In this view, man and society were always hovering on the brink of chaos and could be kept from dissolution and in some semblance of order only by the most rigid and unswerving adherence to the rules that reason had created, no matter how artificial they might be. In both the religious and the philosophical argument, in any case, the state appeared as an essentially punitive or corrective institution, in which all dispute was the beginning of disintegration and obedience to a single authority, the only method of preservation.

The political and social history of the sixteenth and seventeenth centuries provided the most telling practical argument for absolute monarchy. Civil and international wars, religious conflict, social revolts, and the general uncertainty of life in this most unstable early modern Europe produced numerous political treatises that spoke of absolute monarchy as the only possible answer to public insecurity and disorder. Machiavelli in Italy, Bodin in

France, Hobbes in England, and many others of lesser fame in other countries wrote of the dissension that must necessarily arise when the essential attributes of sovereignty were exercised by more than one man, and of the peace and order that absolute autocratic rule could bring. It was this argument that, in fact, had worked among various elements of society to bring about such a large degree of social consent to the assertion of the supremacy of royal power within the state, which here, too, was conceived as punitive and was symbolized by the sword of chastisement.

By the second half of the eighteenth century, however, the bases of each of these arguments had been so seriously undermined that they were virtually inadequate to justify the greatly enlarged sphere of authority to which monarchs were now compelled to lay claim if they wished their reform programs to be successful. The progressive secularism of society in a century when religious antagonism was at its lowest ebb since the early sixteenth century had increasingly deprived religious commentary on political affairs, and on the men who guided them, of most of its educated audience, while the progress of enlightened ideas was making great headway in subverting the notion that an innate evil in man made any necessary degree of tyranny virtually a command of God.

Similarly, the chaotic Cartesian cosmos was slowly losing its admirers to the Newtonian universe of discoverable order and law, with the result that monarchy was losing its necessary ordering function to Nature herself. Even the old utilitarian arguments had lost much of their vigor, for the very successes of the punitive absolute monarchy of the sixteenth and seventeenth centuries had made civil war and large-scale rebellions things of the past, had sharply reduced the incidence of brigandage and riots, and had permitted the growth of solid and reasonably prosperous economies. Consequently, the thesis that only absolute monarchy could secure life, property, and peace and order—an excellent argument in the mid-seventeenth century—had become shopworn in the mid-eighteenth; for whenever even the most successful protective measures survive the need that called them into existence, they are usually perceived to be at best superfluous and at worst uncomfortably restrictive.

In the face of the gradual collapse of traditional theoretical arguments for absolute monarchy, the princes of the later eighteenth century were faced with a doubly difficult task: they had to defend not only the traditional sphere of public authority they had inherited from the past, but also a vast increase in their public functions. The means they chose to accomplish this were, significantly, harmonious with the secularism and utilitarianism of the Enlightenment, which, in helping to destroy the old theoretical foundations of their authority, had also provided them with the basis for new ones.

First, nearly all monarchs adopted one or another form of the social contract theory of political authority, according to which government originated as the result of an agreement among men to provide for their needs and wants through the establishment of a common authority. By this theory, as we have already seen, the legitimacy of any form of government was founded on its utility to the governed, seen in the largely materialistic terms of security of life and property. But since it was logically inherent in this doctrine that any form of government that failed to satisfy the needs and wants of the governed by their own definition became illegitimate and therefore, perhaps, subject to rightful dissolution, it was necessary for monarchs to demonstrate not merely that monarchy, but also *hereditary* monarchy, possessed permanent and compelling advantages over other forms of government. Without such proof, their thrones would become theoretically the playthings of one or another form of popular sovereignty.

In providing such proof, they fell back on arguments that were anything but new. Catherine II asserted in the *Instruction* of 1767 that the vastness of the Russian empire would make any form of government other than autocracy positively ruinous. Joseph II called upon the tremendous diversity of his dominions to prove that only a single absolute ruler could hold them together. And Frederick II, in his *Essay on Forms of Government* (1777), seems to suggest that some of the worst dangers to the state lay in struggles over political power, and that only the hereditary principle of monarchy could consistently obviate such struggles. In short, every monarch who adopted the contract theory found some justification for the preservation of hereditary absolute monarchy; but it is important to remember that the abandonment of the theory of monarchy as the indisputable command of a higher religious or philosophical necessity was almost universal, as was the adoption of a strictly utilitarian proof, which sought to justify monarchy in terms of its concrete contribution to social well-being.

Second, the punitive or corrective theory of the function of public authority was more or less definitively abandoned in favor of a welfare theory. Enlightened despotism emphasized to a greater degree than ever before that the true nature of public power included not merely protective or police functions, in the narrow sense of the term, but also a responsibility to foster by active intervention wherever possible a positive increase in the moral, physical, and economic well-being of the people. Neither in theory nor in practice was this an utterly new phenomenon, of course, for even theological-patriarchal conceptions of the duties of rulership, especially since the Reformation, had included injunctions to improve the lot of subjects. What was new was the greater emphasis on the idea that the primary function of government lay not in the sword, but in the helping hand.

Among the many advantages of the welfare theory to princes were its justification of the need for greater state authority (if the welfare of all was to be maximized) and its explanation of the increased interference of the state in the heretofore private sphere of right of individuals and groups (which was necessary for their own and others' well-being). The warfare state, which found it necessary to assert greater authority in order to organize social resources more effectively and therefore to cut more deeply into the hitherto privileged sanctum of private rights, found it possible to justify itself in these actions on the grounds that it was a welfare state. Whether it was a question of pressing beggars into workhouses, interfering in the lord-peasant relationship, or redefining the sphere of authority of the Church, this interventionism easily could be presented as a matter of concern for the welfare of individuals; and if indeed it brought a greater responsibility with it, as it did, princes were only too willing to accept it, because it also brought greater authority. Very true is the statement of a contemporary English historian: "The Welfare State has, in point of fact, very often been closely related to the Warfare State." *

Third, the political thought of enlightened monarchs shows a tendency to abandon the insistence on the sovereignty of the monarchy in favor of the development of another abstraction, "the State." Frederick II was only one of a number of monarchs who fostered a sharp theoretical distinction between the monarch and the state, and who fixed the responsibility of the monarch as "the first servant of the state," its caretaker, trustee, or whatever. In this view, the state thus had an existence apart from and above the monarch himself; it constituted both the authority and the formal public apparatus by which society, at any given time, was governed for its own welfare and, as such, was a permanent and necessary implication of the social contract by which all government was established. The theory further posited that the power exercised by the monarch was not a personal attribute, but belonged to the state and was merely utilized for the public good by the monarch as the executor of the state.

The adoption of this theory had enormous advantages for monarchs at this point in the history of Europe. One of them lay in the freedom it gave to princes to expand indefinitely the authority they exercised, but without being subject to the accusation that they were developing tyranny; for, they could assert, it was the power of the state, not of their persons, that was being augmented. It provided them also with a principle for which they had long felt a need, one that permitted them to escape the restrictions of a social position tied closely, too closely, to one class—the aristocracy. A persistent theory of monarchy in Europe was that a sovereign prince was actually only *primus inter pares* ("first among equals"), merely the first nobleman of the realm. Throughout the history of absolutism, monarchs had increasingly deprived this term of its politically restrictive implications, though they had always remained closely associated with the nobility of which they were still technically members.

By the later eighteenth century, however, there were some

* R. J. White, *Europe in the Eighteenth Century* (New York, 1965), p. 203.

good reasons for them to wish to cut the ties that still linked them so closely in the public mind with the aristocracy. One of the best of these reasons was a growing antagonism between various classes whose expression and intensity varied from one country to another, but which existed everywhere in Europe, especially in the western and central regions. The most vigorous antagonism was frequently that between the increasingly politically self-conscious and articulate middle and professional classes, on the one hand, and the aristocracy, on the other, in which such issues as the political monopoly and privileges of the nobility and the oppressive economic effects of an hierarchical society were of particular importance, and which can be documented in a rapidly growing public literature from the 1760's onwards. Monarchs in all countries had too great a stake in domestic tranquillity and in the economic value of the middle class to allow themselves to be too closely associated in the increasingly belligerent bourgeois mind with their social allies in the aristocracy. They found in this new theory of the state a doctrine that permitted them to assert a kind of class neutrality and to appear as the impartial arbiter of all social interests, whose only concern was the welfare of all.

This did not mean that monarchs had given up their devotion to the maintenance of an hierarchical society; none of them did, for they instinctively felt their own thrones tied to it and to the privileges it entailed, and they were careful to preserve it. But their depersonalization of their own role in society gave them the best of two worlds. When it was politically or economically expedient for them to proceed against certain privileges of the upper classes, they could be justified before society by calling on the general interest; but, by the same token, when they wished to confirm other privileges or to preserve the principle of privilege itself, they could do so without being accused of narrow aristocratic class prejudice. The increased talk about merit as a criterion of holding public office illustrates the point: it could be used to justify appointment of commoners to office on the basis of their acquired skills or knowledge, but it could just as easily be employed to justify the monopoly of offices by aristocrats on the basis of their skills of management and command, which were supposedly an attribute of their experience as a privileged class. Thus, arguments to prove the utility of anything could be found and could work, if public confidence were not lacking.

That it was not lacking was not due merely to theory, however, no matter how nicely stated, but also to what rulers did to create conviction that their concern for the state as a public trust was more than mere cant. It began to appear that various rulers were making an effort to establish institutions that would really and formally convert their realms from feudal patrimonies into modern "states." The following things in particular were important in this development:

1. A greater sense of responsibility in the handling of public moneys. This manifested itself as frugality in court expenditures, and indeed almost to the point of a fixation in the case of princes such as Frederick II and Joseph II. The idea that the funds administered by the ruler were public or state funds was given support in various ways in different places: by statements that described crown lands as public lands held in trust; by formal separation of state revenues from the private income of the ruler; and by the beginnings of a sense of responsibility to give some sort of public accounting of state revenues and expenditures.

2. A greater emphasis on the establishment of a permanent state civil service, which implied appointment on merit, the decline of venality and favoritism, and tenure of office during good behavior rather than during the pleasure of the monarch. Imperfectly realized, and in many respects pursued with serious misgivings by rulers themselves, this policy nonetheless did characterize both the stated intent and the actual practice of many rulers.

3. The attempt to create one or another form of known, uniform, and written fundamental law, whether by codification of already existing laws or by the elaboration of new codes, whose integrity would be guaranteed by a judiciary made separate from the administration, and whose members again would hold office during good behavior.

4. Certain tendencies towards the infusion of the monarchical state with the spirit of the *res publica*. This is an elusive development, but it can be seen to some extent in proposals for the

return of certain administrative powers to local groups and in the creation of local or provincial representative advisory assemblies or in plans or proposals to do so. Above all, perhaps, it can be seen in a greater encouragement of individual initiative and voluntarism in commerce, manufacturing, and agriculture, of which a somewhat increased freedom, the fostering of economic societies, and the establishment of popular educational systems provide concrete examples. Specific ethical and ideological underpinnings were given to this voluntarism by several monarchs in writing and public statements that emphasized the necessity for the growth of a confraternity of all citizens devoting themselves to the public welfare. Indeed, there grew up in this period a whole new rhetoric about "citizenship," frequently cited in connection with discussions of its contribution to the high level of public morality and public spirit of the ancient republics of Greece and Rome.

We have seen that each and every one of these tendencies or developments is explicable in terms of its relation to specific economic and political problems that beset monarchs to one degree or another all over Europe after the mid-century or so. But their relationship to one another suggests a higher connection as well. Taken together, they all represent an attempt of monarchs to create constitutions for their states. What did constitution mean to them? A set of interconnected laws, institutions, procedures, and animating ideas, integrated as perfectly with one another as possible, that would function internally with the regularity and dependability of a machine. It would relieve the ruler of the, by now, impossible task of daily supervision of every facet of state administration, but without depriving him of his absolutely commanding position to turn this machine towards whatever goals he might choose. Leopold of Tuscany in the late 1780's recognized the great value of constitution in this respect when he penned an approval of the principle of constitutionalism: "The nation clings to [a constitution] and since it believes that it is governing itself, it is therefore much easier to influence, to govern, and to lead to its welfare and happiness."

Constitution, then, in this specialized meaning of the term, was an almost unavoidable solution to the political dilemma posed to monarchs of the late eighteenth century by their desire to retain mastery of society in a time in which the volume and complexity of state business, already vast and still steadily increasing, made truly personal control an impossibility. Constitution, like a lever, was to be inserted between the mover and the object to be moved —i.e., between the monarch and the state—with the intent to augment the power of the mover. This was, in reality, the novel substance that invested the term "state" with an entirely new significance.

It was only with this kind of state in mind that Frederick II could speak of himself as the first servant of the state. And how new and different this impersonal, yet higher, conception of the state and kingship was from what had preceded it may perhaps be seen by contrast with the *Mémoires* of Louis XIV, gone from the scene only since 1715, where Roman, feudal, and Christian interpretations are blended to form a splendid and awe-inspiring baroque edifice of kingship, magnificently arrogant in its assumption that all that was the state was indeed caught up in the almost divine person of the Sun King himself. Louis never in fact made the statement "L'État c'est moi," which has so often been attributed to him; but it is an assertion completely harmonious with the impression he himself strove to create. In any case, Louis was, at the utmost, a servant only of God; the statement of Frederick II, which posited a civil society prior to and above not only the reigning monarch but the institution of monarchy itself, would have been neither comprehensible nor palatable to Louis.

Here then, perhaps, is the highest meaning of "enlightened despotism" and its most profound significance as an epoch of European history. It was a development made necessary by the implacable growth of societies in population, economic resources, and in their social and political complexity. And, though its full cohesiveness was not always perceived at the time, it was a highly rational answer to a very difficult problem, and one that was entirely worthy of the "enlightenment" to which it owed many of its particulars. The continued vigor of monarchy as a form of government in this period is not least demonstrated by its ability to adapt itself to changing sets of circumstances, and with a large measure of success.

But obviously the success of enlightened despotism varied greatly from one country to another. Those monarchs with the most ambitious or radical reform programs had the least success in results, measured against their goals; Joseph II of Austria is the best example. But even in Austria—and certainly in Spain, Prussia, Russia, Tuscany, and other lesser countries where at least the method of reform was slower and less violent than in the Hapsburg lands—some important results, above all in the economic field, were achieved. It is not possible, generally speaking, in any instance to point to major and permanent transformations in the character of the European states; but it is possible to speak of a successful attempt to remove numerous abuses in public life, of a strengthening of state finances, and, very significantly, of the creation of a kind of public spirit and confidence in the regime that gave monarchy itself an enhanced reputation, especially among the middle classes.

It is traditional, at this point, for the historian to pose the difficult and speculative question of the importance of enlightened despotism in preventing elsewhere in Europe the occurrence of revolution such as that which came to France in 1789 and after. Some obvious points suggest themselves, though we cannot here explore this question very fully. First, the Revolution in France was itself a reform movement that became revolutionary largely because of political failures on the part of the king. In no major country of Europe was the fiscal crisis more serious than in France; and in no country had reform had less success in dealing with this critical situation—not because of the failure of reforms themselves to achieve their goals, but because opposition had forced their recall on a timid king before they could even be tested adequately. The convocation of the Estates-General in 1789 was a reform measure in itself; and had Louis XVI at certain critical points made up his mind to accept from the hands of the Third Estate a reform program that in many respects was similar to those of Turgot, Necker, and Calonne, one might today be able to speak of the success of enlightened despotism in France rather than of the success of revolution.

Monarchs such as Joseph II and Leopold II, who lived long enough to see the early phases of the great revolution in France, were in fact convinced that the program of the National Assembly was quite similar to what they had long since begun to do in their lands. As late as 1799, still largely blind to the political implications of the Revolution, a Prussian official told the French *chargé d'affaires* in Berlin that the beneficial revolution the French had made from below was being brought about slowly in Prussia from above. In the interpretation of contemporaries, therefore, the reforms of enlightened despotism contained many of the same elements as those of the Revolution, and had made the movement from below in other countries unnecessary.

But it is well to remember that, even without reform, probably no country in Europe besides France had enough of the ingredients of revolution in 1789 to have produced one unaided. Nowhere was the fiscal crisis as severe as in France; nowhere were the middle classes so large, so well informed, or so resentful of both fiscal and economic policies; nowhere was a succession of salutary reforms better publicized in their consistent failure; nowhere were the privileged classes better entrenched and outfitted for resistance to the government; and, finally, nowhere was there a more irresolute monarch than Louis XVI. Yet a very good argument could be made to support the contention that the occurrence of revolution in France in the long run forced a more rapid execution of more radical reform from the top in many other countries than would have been the case otherwise, and that the pace of such reform can itself be termed almost "revolutionary." Most states, certainly, underwent greater change in the thirty years from 1790 to 1820 than they had in the same number of years from 1760 to 1790. While much of this change was brought by the crusading French themselves, especially under Napoleon, it may still be possible to assert that, by this standard, even the "enlightened" monarchies did not really avoid revolution at all, but merely underwent it in a way different from that of France.

Still, rulers in these states did keep their thrones, which in this revolutionary age was perhaps no mean accomplishment; and the enlightened despots were partly responsible for it. Their work, in removing some of the worst abuses that restricted private achievement and the conduct of beneficial public policies, created a fund of good will among the lower and middle classes that undoubtedly helped to reduce the effectiveness of radical propaganda during the revolutionary era, and therefore contributed to maintain domestic stability. But the salvation of monarchy was achieved at the expense of its absolutism. This was not immediately apparent to most of the enlightened monarchs, nor even to their immediate successors, who did not have to reap the fatal harvest of the seeds that had unwittingly been sown in the attempt to resolve a political problem in favor of the continued monarchical sovereignty and supremacy within the state. It was to become more and more urgently apparent to their later successors, however, and was to result in a steady erosion of monarchical powers in the nineteenth century in all countries.

By their own adoption of social contract theory, the enlightened monarchs had opened the doors to public discussion of government and political affairs, which were now admitted to be human creations, not divine, and which were therefore subject to the debates that led to truth as much as were any other objects of human utility. By their personal frugality and modest habits, which extended to the point of penury and personal discomfort in the more extreme cases, they also helped to remove the awe and grandeur of their office. Their own attacks on the privileged classes, circumspect and limited though they were, were accompanied by a propaganda of public utility that encouraged men to believe that egalitarianism was legitimate—witness the Prussian official cited above, who in 1799 confidently claimed that within a few years there would no longer be a privileged class in Prussia, and who characterized the king (Frederick William III) as "a democrat in his own way."

Most important, the enlightened despots had created constitutions for their states; in a larger sense, in fact, they had created "the State" as the entity we know today. These self-sufficient and self-regulating constitutional mechanisms for a time saved the monarchs from the fate of "drowning in the inkpot," as Leopold once put it—i.e., from being suffocated under the incredible mass of paper work they otherwise had to deal with to insure that the government of the state was conducted according to their wishes. But like the machine it was intended to be, the State could function as well under one operator as another; its organization was permanent, its institutions ready to respond to the command of whoever or whatever held sovereign power.

The monarchs, whose continual personal guidance had once been necessary to the very cohesion of public life, had now, in short, brought to a certain stage of perfection an institution that made them potentially dispensable, as well as a conception of the supremacy of law to which even they could potentially be regarded as subject. It was sheer necessity that drove them to it, and they were not to suffer greatly from it until the doctrine of undivided popular sovereignty fully established the People as the operator of the machine. But, of course, they had done their share to train this new operator, also. It was entirely appropriate that the one man among the enlightened despots who had the deepest insight and understanding of constitutions, from his own experience of conceiving and writing one, should make the shrewdest assessment of the effect such constitutions were to have on monarchy in the future; said Leopold of Tuscany, evaluating his own vocation: "It is a bankrupt business to be a prince."

Finally, then, "enlightened despotism" appears in historical perspective not only as the end phase of absolute monarchy, in which personal monarchical power created the theoretical and practical foundations for its own transformation into an increasingly depersonalized constitutional power, but also as an important stage in the formation of the modern state, during which a greater political unity was given to states and in which "enlightened" secular and utilitarian theories of political life found a formal and permanent place in governmental practice and the organization of public power. Designed entirely as an expedient, not different in purpose from many others that had been found necessary in the past, the state created by the reforms of the enlightened monarchs ended, over the next century and a half, in making monarchy itself merely an expedient—and, as it developed, one that the European world determined it could do without.

Bibliographical Note

No short bibliography could possibly hope to list the number of works necessary to an even minimally comprehensive survey of enlightened despotism, for any book that deals with the description or analysis of the policies of nearly any European monarchical state after 1750 or so and until the Revolution would be a potential candidate for inclusion. In this case, therefore, the process of selection is a very difficult one; only the most important and directly applicable titles will be used, with an emphasis on general introductions to the problems discussed in the book, and especially on those available in English. The student who wishes a still more detailed list should consult the bibliographies contained in the works cited here. A good general bibliographical guide, for the American student especially, is *The American Historical Association's Guide to Historical Literature* (N.Y., 1961).

GENERAL WORKS FOR THE PERIOD

Useful short surveys of eighteenth-century Europe as a whole are available in some number. Two recent ones are Leonard W. Cowie, *Eighteenth Century Europe* (London, 1962), and R. J. White, *Europe in the Eighteenth Century* (N.Y., 1965). The latter, in particular, devotes some attention to an analysis of enlightened despotism. Leo Gershoy, *From Despotism to Revolution, 1763–1789* (N.Y., 1944) concentrates greater attention on the period of the enlightened monarchs, as does Volume VIII of the New

Cambridge Modern History, *The American and French Revolutions, 1763–93*, edited by A. Goodwin (Cambridge, 1965). Two recent works are of special value for their attempt to set the reforms of the European monarchs in a broad Atlantic context of late eighteenth-century revolution: R. R. Palmer, *The Age of the Democratic Revolutions*, vol. I (Princeton, 1959), and Jacques Godechot, *France and the Atlantic Revolution of the Eighteenth Century, 1770–1799*, translated by Herbert Rowen (N.Y., 1965).

Economic histories covering this period for all of Europe are necessarily rather general, but Herbert Heaton, *Economic History of Europe*, revised edition (N.Y., 1948) and S. B. Clough and C. W. Cole, *An Economic History of Europe*, 3rd edition (Boston, 1952) are both serviceable. B. H. Slicher van Bath, *The Agrarian History of Western Europe, A.D. 500 to 1850*, translated by Olive Ordish (N.Y., 1963) is uniquely valuable. A standard history of economic theory is Erich Roll, *A History of Economic Thought*, revised edition (London, 1946).

THE ENLIGHTENMENT

Among the best surveys of European thought for this period are the two volumes by Paul Hazard, *The European Mind, 1680–1715* (New Haven, 1953), and *European Thought in the Eighteenth Century* (New Haven, 1954), both translated by J. Lewis May. Daniel Mornet's *French Thought in the Eighteenth Century*, translated by Lawrence Levin (N.Y., 1929), though narrower in scope, is also excellent. The standard work on the metaphysical foundations of eighteenth-century thought is Ernst Cassirer, *The Philosophy of the Enlightenment*, translated by Fritz Koelln and James Pettegrove (Princeton, 1951). A shorter but very competent survey is by Alfred Cobban, *In Search of Humanity: the Role of the Enlightenment in Modern History* (London, 1960). Franklin L. Baumer, *Religion and the Rise of Scepticism* (N.Y., 1960), contains a good discussion of the central role of religious ideas in the growth of enlightened social criticism.

The great influence of French thought in the European enlightenment as a whole makes the famous work of Kingsley Martin, *French Liberal Thought in the Eighteenth Century*, 2nd edition, edited by J. P. Mayer (London, 1962), of more extensive value than its title suggests; the same is true of Peter Gay, *The Party of Humanity: Essays in the French Enlightenment* (N.Y., 1964). Professor Gay has also made a major contribution to the social and political thought of the *philosophes* through his analysis of *Voltaire's Politics: the Poet as Realist* (N.Y., 1965). Henry Vyverberg, *Historical Pessimism in the French Enlightenment* (Cambridge, Mass., 1958) is a good corrective to the usual view of the *philosophes* as unrelieved optimists.

Physiocracy has a considerable literature. In English, an old book by Henry Higgs, *The Physiocrats* (N.Y., 1897; reprinted, Hamden, Conn., 1963), though quite out of date, is still the best survey. Ronald Meek, *The Economics of Physiocracy* (London, 1962) has reprinted extracts from a number of Physiocratic works, and contains an excellent short interpretation of Physiocratic doctrine. Mario Einaudi, *The Physiocratic Doctrine of Judicial Control* (Cambridge, Mass., 1938) attempts to explore one of the most interesting political ramifications of Physiocratic theory. In French, three works by the eminent Georges Weulersse give by far the best overall account of the movement: *Le mouvement physiocratique en France (de 1756 à 1770)*, 2 vols. (Paris, 1910); *Les Physiocrats* (Paris, 1931); and *La Physiocratie sous les ministères de Turgot et Necker (1774–1781)* (Paris, 1950).

Two special aspects of enlightened thought that are of particular importance to enlightened despotism have been treated in James Heath, *Eighteenth Century Penal Theory* (Oxford, 1963), which contains extracts from major works of the period; and John W. Gough, *The Social Contract: A Critical Study of its Development* (Oxford, 1936).

ENLIGHTENED DESPOTISM

The number of studies devoted to enlightened despotism as a distinct historical phenomenon is not large. The most massive study so far undertaken is that of the international committee, the work of whose members, covering various topics and countries of Europe in a somewhat helter-skelter fashion, may be found in *Bulletin of the International Committee of Historical Science,* vol. 1 (1928), pp. 601–12; vol. 2 (1930), pp. 533–52; vol. 5 (1933), pp. 701–804; and vol. 9 (1937), pp. 2–131, 135–225, 519–37. The study of Geoffrey Bruun, *The Enlightened Despots* (N.Y., 1929) is short, anecdotal, and outdated. Fritz Hartung, *Enlightened Despotism*, translated and revised by H. Otto and G. Barraclough (London, 1957) is an abbreviated but excellent analysis and interpretation, though concerned almost exclusively with Prussia. Other analyses available in English include Georges Lefebvre, "Enlightened Despotism," *The Development of the Modern State*, edited by Heinz Lubasz (N.Y., 1964), pp. 48–64, which glimpses much hypocrisy behind the reforms of the enlightened monarchs; and Charles Morazé, "The Domestic Policies of Frederick the Great, Catherine the Great, Maria Theresa, and Joseph II," *The European Past: Reappraisals in History from the Renaissance through Waterloo*, edited by S. B. Clough *et al.*, vol. I (N.Y., 1964), pp. 375–94, which analyzes the public finance of a number of sovereigns.

Two especially interesting theoretical articles that attempt to relate the peculiarities of enlightened despotism to the development of new theories of state and society are Ernst Walder, "Zwei Studien über den aufgeklärten Absolutismus," *Schweizer Beiträge zur allgemeinen Geschichte*, vol. 15 (1957), pp. 134–71; and Heinz Holldack, "Der Physiokratismus und die absolute Monarchie," *Historische Zeitschrift*, vol. 145 (1931), pp. 517–49.

PARTICULAR AREAS AND RULERS

Most of the historical literature applicable to a topic such as enlightened despotism actually falls into the category of national or regional history and biography, and must therefore be dealt with by particular countries and monarchs. Again, because of the vastness of the general topic, the selection must be very stringent, and is aimed primarily at the general reader.

Germany: Prussia and Austria

The best general survey of German history for this entire period in English will be found in Hajo Holborn, *A History of Modern Germany*, vol. II (1648–1840) (N.Y., 1963). A balanced social history of the eighteenth century is provided by W. H. Bruford, *Germany in the Eighteenth Century: the Social Background of the Literary Revival* (Cambridge, 1935), while Frederick Hertz, *The Development of the German Public Mind*, vol. II (The Enlightenment) (London, 1962) gives an interesting history of public opinion, politics, and social development in eighteenth-century Germany, with considerable attention to Frederick II, Maria Theresa, and Joseph II. The first few chapters of Leonard Krieger, *The German Idea of Freedom: History of a Political Tradition* (Boston, 1957) are quite valuable as analyses of the development of the theory of enlightened despotism in Germany. Helen P. Liebel, *Enlightened Bureaucracy versus Enlightened Despotism in Baden, 1750–1792* (Philadelphia, 1965) is a pioneering attempt to analyze the role of bureaucrats in the elaboration of reform projects in one small German state. The educational theory and practice of enlightened despotism is illuminated by Andreas Flitner's important work, *Die politische Erziehung in Deutschland: Geschichte und Probleme, 1750–1880* (Tübingen, 1957), while the beginnings of political sectarianism and ferment in Germany are ably discussed in Fritz Valjavec, *Die Entstehung der politischen Strömungen in Deutschland, 1770–1815* (Munich, 1951).

The best introduction to Frederick II of Prussia in English is G. P. Gooch, *Frederick the Great: the Ruler, the Writer, the Man* (N.Y., 1947), but it does not compare in scope or depth of analysis to the great work of R. Koser, *König Friedrich der Grosse*, 4 vols. (Stuttgart, 1912), which is a model of political biography. Particularly important aspects of Prussian history in the eighteenth century pertaining to enlightened despotism are treated by Walter Dorn, "The Prussian Bureaucracy in the Eighteenth Century," *Political Science Quarterly*, vol. 46 (1931), pp. 403–23; vol. 47 (1932), pp. 75–94, 259–73; and by Hans Rosenberg, *Bureaucracy, Autocracy, and Aristocracy: the Prussian Experience, 1660–1815* (Cambridge, Mass., 1958), whose explication of socio-political relationships is of great importance to an understanding of Prussian internal policy in the eighteenth century. Herman Weill's *Frederick the Great and Samuel von Cocceji: A Study in the Reform of the Prussian Judicial Administration, 1740–1755* (Madison, Wisc., 1961) helps to explain the nature of legal and judicial reform, while W. O. Henderson's valuable *Studies in the Economic Policy of Frederick the Great* (London, 1963) demonstrates the extraordinary vigor, if not always the wisdom, of Frederick's economic thought and policy.

The best studies of Joseph II are by Saul K. Padover, *The Revolutionary Emperor, Joseph the Second, 1741–1790* (N.Y., 1934), and Francois Fejtö, *Joseph II, Kaiser und Revolutionär: ein Lebensbild* (Stuttgart, 1956). The reign of Maria Theresa is not well covered by any book in English; the most useful and scholarly treatment is still Eugen Guglia, *Maria Theresia, ihr Leben und ihre Regierung*, 2 vols. (Munich, 1917). Fritz Valjavec, *Der Josephinismus: zur geistigen Entwicklung Oesterreichs im 18. und 19. Jahrhundert*, 2nd edition (Munich, 1945) is an original attempt to sketch the outlines of the effects of the Austrian enlightenment on the political and social history of the country. A good cultural background for the reform period after 1740 can be obtained in Robert Kann, *A Study in Austrian Intellectual History: from Late Baroque to Romanticism* (N.Y., 1960). An Italian work, Franco Valsecchi's *L'assolutismo illuminato in Austria e in Lombardia*, 2 vols. (Bologna, 1931–34) is particularly valuable for its discussion of Lombard reforms, while the Bohemian lands and their relationship to the Austrian crown, primarily under Leopold II, are the subject of a detailed treatment by Robert J. Kerner, *Bohemia in the Eighteenth Century* (N.Y., 1932). An excellent recent political biography of Leopold is that of Adam Wandruszka, *Leopold II*, 2 vols. (Vienna, 1964–65).

Scandinavia

A most serviceable general introduction to all of Scandinavia for the period is B. J. Hovde, *The Scandinavian Countries, 1720–1865*, vol. I (The Rise of the Middle Classes) (Ithaca, N.Y., 1948), which emphasizes the unity of historical experience of the Scandinavian countries. The best history of Sweden in English is Ingvar Anderson, *A History of Sweden*, translated by Carolyn Hannay (N.Y., 1956). No adequate treatment of Gustavus III appears anywhere in English, though an old work by Robert N. Bain, *Gustavus III and his Contemporaries, 1746–1792*, 2 vols.

(London, 1894) is a creditable attempt to place the enlightened monarch in the literary and intellectual context of late eighteenth-century Sweden. The most recent Swedish biography is by Beth Hennings, *Gustav III* (Stockholm, 1957). For economic developments, Eli Heckscher's *An Economic History of Sweden*, translated by Göran Ohlin (Cambridge, Mass., 1954), is an excellent survey.

The history of Denmark is presented in brief compass by Palle Lauring, *A History of the Kingdom of Denmark*, translated by David Hohnen (Copenhagen, 1960), and by John Danstrup, *A History of Denmark*, 2nd edition (Copenhagen, 1949). Probably still the most reliable study of Struensee is by Josef Magnus Wehner, *Struensee* (Munich, 1925).

Spain and Portugal

The somewhat outdated approach of Rafael Altamira, *A History of Spain from the Beginnings to the Present Day*, translated by Muna Lee (N.Y., 1949), does not detract from its value as a social and cultural survey; its deficiencies are balanced by the more political and institutional approach of Harold V. Livermore, *A History of Spain* (London, 1958). The best overall institutional history remains the work of Georges N. Desdevises du Dezert, *L'Espagne de l'ancien régime*, 3 vols. (Paris, 1897–1905). Antonio Dominguez Ortiz, *La sociedad española en el siglo XVIII* (Madrid, 1955), gives a good account of economic developments.

For the subject of enlightened despotism, an excellent and indispensable book is Richard Herr, *The Eighteenth Century Revolution in Spain* (Princeton, 1958). A French study of great merit is Jean Sarrailh, *L'Espagne éclairée de la seconde moitié du XVIIIe siècle* (Paris, 1954). Robert Jones Shafer, *The Economic Societies in the Spanish World, 1763–1821* (Syracuse, N.Y., 1958), and Julius Klein, *The Mesta: A Study in Spanish Economic History, 1273–1836* (Cambridge, Mass., 1920) are studies of important institutions in the development of the Spanish economy in the eighteenth century.

There is a dearth of English materials on the history of Portugal. The English reader will find Charles E. Nowell, *A History of Portugal* (Princeton, 1958) and Harold V. Livermore, *A History of Portugal* (Cambridge, 1947) brief and unexciting.

The only English-language biography of Pombal is by Marcus Cheke, *Dictator of Portugal: A Life of Marquis de Pombal, 1699–1782* (London, 1938), which is a personal, rather than a political, biography and has little to say about Pombal's important reforms.

France

Among the best short French accounts of the eighteenth century is Philippe Sagnac, *La formation de la société française moderne*, vol. II (La révolution des idées et des moeurs et le declin de l'ancien régime, 1715–1788) (Paris, 1946), which is strong in both analysis and interpretation. G. P. Gooch, *Louis XV: The Monarchy in Decline* (London and N.Y., 1956) is a good account in English. For the later period, Saul K. Padover, *The Life and Death of Louis XVI* (N.Y., 1939) is uneven and not up to the standard of the author's work on Joseph II.

Roger Bickart, *Les parlements et la notion de souveraineté au XVIIIe siècle* (Paris, 1932) is a fine introduction to the relationship of *parlements* and crown during the eighteenth century, while Franklin Ford, *Robe and Sword: the Regrouping of the French Aristocracy after Louis XIV* (Cambridge, Mass., 1953) is a brilliant study of the causes of aristocratic solidarity in the years preceding the Revolution. Douglas Dakin, *Turgot and the Ancien Régime in France* (London, 1939) is a kind of political biography of the famous reformer and controller-general, which also examines the role of intendants and the failure of reform in late eighteenth-century France. Two interesting monographs on subjects closely related to the interpretation of enlightened despotism in France are Lester B. Mason, *The French Constitution and the Social Question in the Old Regime, 1700–1789* (Buffalo, 1954), and George T. Matthews, *The Royal General Farms in Eighteenth Century France* (N.Y., 1958). Shelby T. McCloy provides an important background for much of the movement of social reform in *The Humanitarian Movement in Eighteenth Century France* (Lexington, Ky., 1957).

Italy

After the successful and time-tested brief survey by Janet P. Trevelyan, *A Short History of the Italian People from the Bar-*

barian Invasions to the Present Day, 4th edition (London and N.Y., 1956), the English reader will find himself virtually without resources for the eighteenth century in Italy. Some general history is available in Emiliana P. Noether, *Seeds of Italian Nationalism, 1700–1815* (N.Y., 1951), although the focus of the book is largely restricted to political nationalism. Ettore Rota, *Le origini del Risorgimento (1700–1800),* 2nd revised edition, 2 vols. (Milan, 1948) is the best Italian history of the eighteenth century, though the one-volume study by Franco Valsecchi, *L'Italia nel settecento dal 1714 al 1788* (Milan, 1959) is also very useful. We have already mentioned Valsecchi's valuable study on enlightened despotism in Lombardy in the Austrian section, as well as Adam Wandruszka's biography of Leopold II, much of which deals with his reign as Grand Duke of Tuscany. Luigi Bulferetti, *L'assolutismo illuminato in Italia (1700–1789)* (Milan, 1944) is primarily a source book, but with an excellent introduction and notes.

Russia

There are a large number of recent and competent general histories of Russia in English. Of the one-volume histories, Nicholas V. Riasonovsky, *A History of Russia* (N.Y., 1963) is quite good. Michael T. Florinsky, *Russia: A History and an Interpretation,* 2 vols. (N.Y., 1953) is a longer survey. There is no really first-rate political biography of Catherine II; the best of a bad lot are probably: Henry Valloton, *Catherine II* (Paris, 1955), in French; and in English, Ian Grey, *Catherine the Great: Autocrat and Empress of All Russia* (London, 1961); and an old favorite, Edward A. B. Hodgetts, *The Life of Catherine the Great of Russia* (London, 1914). The enlightened characteristics of Catherine II and the text of the *Instruction* of 1767 may be found in the source book of William F. Reddaway, editor, *Documents of Catherine the Great: the Correspondence with Voltaire and the Instruction of 1767* (Cambridge, 1931).

The economic history of Petr I. Liashchenko, *History of the National Economy of Russia to the 1917 Revolution* (N.Y., 1949) is the most recent comprehensive, though also semi-official, study; but the work of Josef M. Kulischer, *Russische Wirtschaftsgeschichte* (Jena, 1925) still has much value. Some of the educational innovations and changes of Russian enlightened despotism can be traced in Nicholas A. Hans, *History of Russian Educational Policy, 1701–1917* (London, 1931). The best study of the famous legislative commission of 1767 is Georg Sacke, *Die gesetzgebende Kommission Katharinas II: ein Beitrag zur Geschichte des Absolutismus in Russland* (Breslau, 1940).

Index

113